Endorsements

"When a successful person has 45 years of experience, and chooses to boil all he knows down to the essence, it is wise to pay attention. In this book, one of the most successful coaches I have ever known promises to mentor you into an elevated version of yourself. I think it is a must read."

–Robert E. Quinn, Author of *The Positive Organization*

"When Rob Pasick speaks, people listen...and when he writes, people want to read it...and that's because Rob has a clear mission in mind with all his words...he wants to help people put everything in their lives in perspective, in the proper place.

"Self-Aware: A Guide for Success in Work and Life is a book that is clear, concise and easy to understand. It will make a difference in how you balance your professional and personal life and it may make a difference in what you end up doing. I have known Rob for years, and he is a wise and caring and ever so smart man who wants to guide young men and women, helping them to be the best they can be. Rob really cares and puts so much thought into realistic ways to have professional success and personal happiness. This is a book you won't want to miss!"

–Cheryl Chodun, former TV news reporter, WXYZ, Detroit and Adjunct Professor at Madonna University.

"Rob Pasick did it—this workbook makes his popular university course readily accessible to young professionals. His expertise as an executive coach is translated to early career principles that will serve the reader for decades to come."

–Michelle Machiele, M.A., Educational Leadership, Teaching Assistant, University of Michigan Ross School of Business, 2015

Self-Aware

A Guide for Success in Work and Life

by Robert Pasick, Ph.D.
with Dunrie Greiling, Ph.D.

Copyright and Contact Info

Thank you
to
Pat,
Adam and Sarah,
&
Dan and Katrina.

Contents

About this Book

In over 45 years as a practicing psychologist, social entrepreneur, and professor, I have learned that emotional intelligence is the key to success in work and in life. I also know that becoming more self-aware is the key to developing strong emotional intelligence.

I have taught, coached, and counseled people on how to become more self-aware and how to develop their social emotional competencies. Both activities lead to higher emotional intelligence.

This book presents the best practices developed and delivered in my teaching and in my psychology practice. Some of the stories and exercises in this book came from my previous book *Balanced Leadership in Unbalanced Times* (2009). I published some of the stories and exercises as articles on my blog at RobPasick.com. Please visit as I will continue to write there.

I wrote this book because not everyone who needs this information is here at the University of Michigan to take my class. While it's nice to have a teacher and coach to help you through the process, you can learn a lot by yourself through reading this book and working on its exercises.

If you follow the process, you'll end up with a self-made vision for success in both work and life. Furthermore, you will learn to set goals and develop the support that will enable you to make your dreams come true.

Genesis of this Book

Three years ago I had the opportunity to teach a course to seniors at the University of Michigan Ross School of Business on the topic of Managing Professional Relationships in the Workplace. As I developed the curriculum, I focused on the importance of emotional intelligence and interpersonal skills as keys to success in work. Over the past three years, I've continued to teach the course at Ross. Then, the Michigan Center for Entrepreneurship at the University of Michigan College of Engineering approached me to teach a similar course to graduate students in science, technology, engineering, and math (STEM), and I gladly accepted the challenge.

I hear from my students that they are interested in exploring a more holistic perspective on their lives. They're interested in taking control of their time and lives as they pursue a happy and healthy lifestyle. They tell me they are not just interested in doing well in their careers, but they want to achieve well-being in their lives and to make their world a better place.

In response to my students' deep need, I developed the class as a process where my students look deeply at themselves to reflect upon who they are and what they want from their lives. It is not merely a self-reflective process. They also are encouraged to share and interact with others weekly.

Through the thirteen weeks of the course, my students go through a series of exercises that take them on a path of self-discovery toward improved emotional intelligence. They work individually and participate in small collaborative groups. They also interview young and successful business leaders about their lives and careers.

At the end of class, each student creates a personal development plan with a five-year vision of what they want to achieve. In addition to career success, my students are asked to describe what they hope to achieve in other important aspects of their life, including relationships, health and well-being, and community service. The final project is to present this plan to the class and to get feedback and help from their classmates about how to achieve their goals.

This book is designed to take the reader through a similar process. By reading and doing the exercises, you will:

- Gain a better sense of self-awareness.
- Develop your emotional intelligence competency.
- Craft a personal vision for success in career and life.
- Set goals to help you achieve a good life.
- Learn how to achieve these goals.
- Plan how to create a team to help you in the pursuit of your goals.

Target Audience

I have based the material on two courses I teach at the University of Michigan on the topic of interpersonal relationships and career planning. One class is for college seniors and the other is offered to graduate students in the STEM fields.

While the process I describe in this book may be applied by everyone who is contemplating career or school choices, this particular book is designed for college students and people early in their career.

Warning!
This Book Could Change Your Life!

From a student:

> *"Before being a part of this class, I thought I knew exactly what I wanted to do and which career path I wanted to embark on.*
>
> *"However, after hearing some of the guest speakers and through immense self-reflection, I found that my passions lay elsewhere and I needed to develop a new plan of action.*
>
> *"I have always been passionate about fashion, yet I always thought that I did not have what it takes to be successful in this industry. Hearing from guest speakers has inspired me and given me the courage to follow my passion and embrace the risk."*
>
> *–Sydney Tucker*

If you are not ready to make significant changes in your life, my advice is not to read this book. Keep this book in a safe space for another day. My students often report that through the processes in this workbook, they have switched from one career path to another.

Here are my warnings:

- Do not read this book if you do not want to seriously reexamine your career path.
- Do not read this book if you are unwilling to confront ways in which you are neglecting your well-being.
- Do not read this book if you are not willing to talk to other people about yourself.
- Do not read this book if you are uncomfortable aligning your mission and values with your life choices.

Be brave.

"I am what I am, an' I'm not ashamed."
-Rubeus Hagrid, from Harry Potter and the Goblet of Fire by J.K. Rowling

How to Use this Book

This book reflects the process I use in my coaching and teaching. If followed, you will embark on a process designed to increase your self-awareness. You will be asked to read, reflect, answer questions, and engage actively in a series of exercises. Some exercises will require the participation of significant people in your life.

You will be guided through exercises designed to:

- Help you find your career sweet spot.
- Establish a vivid vision of your dream success in career and life.
- Establish goals in the key spheres of your life: family, friends, mind, body, spirit, career, and community.
- Determine how the right balance in these spheres will lead to choices that maximize your chances to be happy and successfully choose the right mate.
- Better understand others.
- Better manage your relationship with yourself.
- Better manage your relationship with others.

Workbook Structure and Summary

This workbook contains questions and exercises designed to help you better understand yourself. This book contains thirteen chapters in three parts. Plan to schedule two chapters a week to complete the process.

Part One is the introduction and framework.

- Chapter 1 - From Self-Awareness to Emotional Intelligence.

Part Two contains seven chapters, each on a theme within Self Discovery.

- Chapter 2 - Self-Discovery Step One: Discover Your Strengths.
- Chapter 3 - Self-Discovery Step Two: Uncover Your Interests and Passions. Interests and passions are key to selecting a profession.
- Chapter 4 - Self-Discovery Step Three: Understand Your Personality. Research has consistently shown that there are five basic components of personality. You will learn what these are and how you can assess your own personal style.
- Chapter 5 - Self-Discovery Step Four: Manage Your Energy and Your Body.
- Chapter 6 - Self-Discovery Step Five: Care for Your Mind.
- Chapter 7 - Self-Discovery Step Six: Invest in Your Relationships. You will explore what you need to understand about yourself, to determine intentional friendships in general, and your significant other in particular.
- Chapter 8 - Self-Discovery Step Seven: Define Your Mission and Core Values.

Part Three asks you to "put it all together."

- Chapter 9 - Map your Lifestyle Values. In this chapter, you will prioritize your values (including how much money you need to support yourself).
- Chapter 10 - Describe Your Career Sweet Spot.
- Chapter 11 - Envision Your Success.
- Chapter 12 - Set Your Goals and Harness Your Willpower.
- Chapter 13 - Create Your Personal Development Plan and Graduate.

This book contains summaries of research and stories from my clients, my students, and my own life.

Some chapter sections and assignments link out to online resources such as assessments, articles, and videos. We have made sure that these links work at the time of publication, but the links may stop working at any time due to changes on third-party sites. Please visit RobPasick.com for an up-to-date resource list.

Your Reflections

Many of the topics are followed by reflection questions, "Your Reflections." The reflection questions are meant to be thought-starters. Not all reflection questions will apply to you, so feel free to choose reflections while challenging yourself.

Your Assignment

For most topics, you'll also have an assignment, "Your Assignment." It will look like this section!

You will benefit from the assignments, so make the time to invest in your personal growth.

Many assignments will go into your Personal Development Plan. It will give you a working document for continued goal-setting and reflection. You may download our Personal Development plan template as a Google doc online. You will need to copy the document so that you can edit and customize your plan. goo.gl/NIWVzu

Enjoy the process!

CHAPTER ONE
From Self-Awareness
to Emotional Intelligence

From a Student

"This class has forced me to speak up more, and from that, I want to start fresh and create a new image for myself, showing that I am a knowledgeable person who is not afraid of speaking up. I want to be able to be recognized for my work and take more responsibility to help me grow as a person. Being able to get out of my comfort zone earlier in my career will help me succeed further down the line."
–Manaswee Malugari

Statement of Principles

Here are the core principles of this book:

- **Self-awareness is step number one and the cornerstone of emotional intelligence**. Without adequate self-awareness, we struggle to understand others, to manage ourselves, and to develop healthy relationships.
- **Self-awareness is a process**. Because the world around us is engaged in continuous change, and because we are forever changing, we never finish developing our own sense of self-awareness.
- **Self-awareness is never wholly about the self**. We mostly learn about ourselves in relation to others.
- **No one succeeds alone**. All major accomplishments occur within a system of cooperation and competition.
- **To learn who we are, we have to act upon the world by trying things**. We learn by action, by making mistakes, and by learning from these mistakes. We cannot become self-aware solely through self-reflection. We must act upon our world to learn from it.

A good, successful life begins with self-awareness.

Self-Awareness and Emotional Intelligence are the Keys to Success

Know Thyself.
−Socrates

Sages throughout history and across cultures have urged us to be self-aware, and thereby understand our world. Modern psychological sciences have consistently reinforced the idea that well-being begins with self-awareness.

One key example of this insight comes from modern psychological research dedicated to emotional intelligence. Beginning with Professor David McClelland, for whom I was a teaching assistant at Harvard University, and continuing through the research of my classmates, Daniel Goleman and Rick Boyatzis, it has been shown that self-awareness is the cornerstone of emotional intelligence. In order to understand other people, we must first understand ourselves. In order to manage any relationship, we must possess self-awareness and other awareness. In order to manage our emotions, we must first understand ourselves. And to manage the complexity of complicated relationships, such as those we find in family, school, teams or work, we must first understand ourselves in relationship to others.

What Are the Emotional Intelligence Competencies?

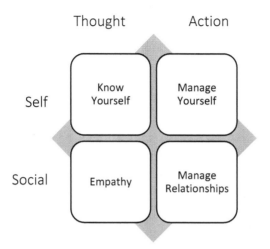

Emotional Intelligence competencies can be thought of as a grid of four squares. In this grid, the self is on top and your social interactions are below.

On the left are the thinking competencies: know yourself, be aware of others. On the right are action competencies: manage yourself and manage relationships.

Key Questions to Ask Yourself on Emotional Intelligence

Here are some questions to ask yourself about your level of emotional intelligence. For each set of questions, there are a few options to increase your competence.

How well do I know myself?

- What are my strengths?
- What are my core values?
- What are my mission and purpose?
- What are my passions and interests?
- What are my blind spots?
- What are the keys to my personality?

To enhance self-awareness
- Practice some form of self-reflection: meditate or pray, write about your feelings, talk to others about your feelings and listen, really listen, to their feedback.
- Set goals – know what you want and where you want to go.

How well do I understand others?

- Do I know how others feel?
- Can I feel how others feel?
- How well do I seek to understand others?
- How well do I read individual differences?
- How sensitive am I to the feelings of others?
- How well do I understand myself in relation to others?

To enhance empathy
- Practice active listening: not debating, not defending, and not counter-attacking.
- Seek first to understand rather than to be understood.

How well do I manage my emotions and my actions?

- How well do I handle stress?
- How well do I manage anger?
- Do I know what I "say to myself" about difficult situations?
- Can I talk myself down from getting upset?
- Can I manage my moods?
- Do I know how to get myself out of a bad mood?
- How well do I manage my time?
- How well do I take care of myself (mind and body)?

To enhance self-management

- Be aware of emotional flooding: the moment your emotions trump your ability to think.
- Be aware of faulty thinking. Bad ideas can lead to bad action. Example bad ideas include: I must be right all the time. I must never admit vulnerability. I must be loved and approved of by everybody, all the time.
- Avoid counter-attacking.
- Practice delaying gratification.

How well do I display empathy toward others?

- How well do I display understanding towards others?
- How well are you able to express your feelings?
- How positive are you with others?
- How well do you exercise good self-restraint when dealing with difficult situations?
- Personal and professional elevator pitch: How do I introduce myself to people I meet?
- How are you at asking good questions of others?
- How well do you actively listen to the answers?

- How are you at sustaining long-term relationships (family, social, personal, professional)?
- How would you rate your ability to influence others?
- How would you rate your ability to lead others?

To manage relationships
- Know it's not always about you.
- Realize we are all on key personality spectra and may need different amounts of time or rationale for decisions.

Emotional Intelligence: An Example

Emotional intelligence is the best predictor of long-term success in the workplace. Research has shown that emotional intelligence is the key factor in the ability of individuals to get along well in relationships. The technology-focused generation of millennials will see this play out in the span of their careers: emotional intelligence is valued even more than intellectual intelligence and technical skills.

Many leaders tend to be competitive, hard-driving people. They have high IQs, but sometimes their emotional intelligence lags far behind.

A few years ago, I coached a manager who had been one of the most successful salespeople at a financial services company. She'd been promoted to manager and was poised to move up to the next level. But as I worked with her, I quickly saw that she lacked the ability to connect well with others.

One of the dimensions of emotional intelligence is whether you are aware of your own feelings. This woman always put on a happy face. If you asked her how she was doing, she'd always say, "Perfect!" She wasn't attuned to the subtleties of her own emotional life because she'd taught herself to simply put on a positive front.

She also wasn't able to read the emotions of others well. She had no sense of the impact her words might have. She'd do things like overdo teasing to the point where it became offensive.

She also was weak on her ability to manage her emotions. She could fly off the handle in an instant and would make no attempt to rein herself in. In fact, she thought yelling at people was the way to motivate them. Instead, people became afraid of her.

She also fell down on her ability to manage the emotions of the group, which is one of the most difficult things to do. Much of the work of leaders involves managing a team or a meeting. It's almost like being an orchestra conductor – sensing how the group is feeling, knowing when to call on someone, recognizing who hasn't been participating. Drawing people out is a delicate art. My client could manage these situations at times, but then she'd have a major blow-up and publicly humiliate someone.

To help her improve her emotional intelligence, I gave her the following suggestions:

- Keep a mood log. Several times a day, write down how you are feeling. Look back at the end of the week and assess how tuned in you were to your own emotions. Look for patterns.
- Avoid shaming others. It can be highly destructive. You may be aware that shaming is destructive to others; you must be aware that shaming is destructive to your reputation.
- At work or at home, make a point of empathizing with others. Put yourself in that person's shoes. Think about what it would feel like to be that person.
- If you're having a dispute, look at it from the other person's viewpoint. Try writing out a narrative of the disagreement from the other person's standpoint.

After six months of coaching, she was able to improve the way she led her team. She gained an increased self-awareness and learned how to manage her emotions better. The feedback from her team was positive and suggested that she had learned how to treat her team members much more respectfully.

Summary Assignment for Emotional Intelligence

Watch my video on emotional intelligence. youtu.be/4Qfx_aFLfhw[1]

Take the online assessment "Do You Lead with Emotional Intelligence" at Harvard Business Review. hbr.org/2015/06/quiz-yourself-do-you-lead-with-emotional-intelligence

Do the results surprise you?

Follow their instructions to get feedback from others. Did their feedback surprise you?

Reflect and write up what you learned in your Personal Development Plan (template available online). I suggest four paragraphs: one on each aspect of emotional intelligence. You might start with this prompt to start each paragraph: I rate myself _____ on _____...

---

[1] You may find it easier to find and follow links like this from the resource page for the book on RobPasick.com.

CHAPTER TWO
Self-Discovery Step One: Discover Your Strengths

From a Student

"The Gallup Strengths Finder revealed my 5 top strengths: ideation, input, restorative, deliberative, and learner.

"Overall, these strengths were accurate as were the tailored descriptions that were provided. I identify most strongly with the ideation, input, deliberative, and learner strengths. I was unsure about the restorative strength until I talked with my wife and reread the description. The restorative strength is about problem solving, which I had overlooked until my wife pointed out that I often try to solve problems that she would get discouraged by. These strengths are likely what drew me to pursue a PhD. I enjoy brainstorming and would much rather come up with new ideas than try to communicate things I already know or learned elsewhere. I have a voracious appetite for information, which ties directly to input and learner. I read a lot, collect data from my experiments, and observe.

"My strengths all conversely result in blind spots. One such blind spot I have always had difficulty expressing my ideas linearly. I tend to make abstract, logical jumps and get frustrated when people are unable to follow my ideas. This class helped me realize that different people have different learning styles. I prefer ideas, while others prefer facts. To address my blind spot, I need to remember to connect the dots between my ideas and support them with examples to help other people better understand me. The converse of the deliberative strength is perfectionism. I have tendency to keep sewing up loose ends in my work to the point of diminishing marginal return on my time."

–a student

Discover Your Strengths

Everyone has a unique set of strengths and abilities, and the more time you spend using these unique talents, the more successful and satisfied you're likely to be. I often employ several methods to get my students and clients to come to a deeper understanding of their talents.

After using one of these methods, I counsel my students and clients to work with the top five strengths they've identified. It's a comfortable number for goal setting.

One of the easiest methods—**and one I've turned to many times**—was developed by Dan Sullivan, founder of StrategicCoach.com. Dan advocates you send e-mails to the people who know you best. Explain that you're going through a leadership development process and ask them to describe your unique strengths, talents and contributions.

I've found that the responses people get are fairly consistent. It shouldn't be too surprising because, for most of us, certain threads weave through our lives. Back in grade school, if you were always organizing neighborhood games or teams, chances are you're still doing it in some fashion at 20, 30, 40 or 50 years of age.

A similar exercise was developed by my colleagues at the Center for Positive Organizations at the University of Michigan's Ross School of Business. As with Sullivan's approach, you request positive feedback from people who know you. Then you use this information to create a portrait of your "best self." You can find out more and purchase the Reflected Best Self exercise online. positiveorgs.bus.umich.edu/cpo-tools/reflected-best-self-exercise-2nd-edition

Another great tool is the Internet-based StrengthsFinder Profile, created by Donald O. Clifton, Tom Rath and a team of scientists from the Gallup Organization. It was later renamed the Clifton StrengthsFinder. When you buy the book or purchase the assessment on the website, you get an access code so you can take the assessment online. The program analyzes your answers and comes up with the five most powerful themes you display. Based on that, you receive action plans and other activities designed to help you understand how best to use your strengths. Here's where to find out more: StrengthsFinder.com

Your Assignment

Either do the Sullivan exercise or use the Reflected Best Self template. Send the messages to important people in your life (coaches, mentors, friends, people with whom you've worked or played) and get their feedback on your strengths.

Purchase the StrengthsFinder 2.0 book and assessment test from the Gallup organization. Then take the test.

Then, fill in the "Strengths" Row in your Personal Development Plan (template available online) with your top five strengths.

Your Special Gift

Ask yourself:
- What is my special gift?
- Am I using my gift to my fullest capacity?
- What do I need to do today, to ensure I have the opportunity to use my gift fully in the future?

I was inspired to consider these questions upon hearing a presentation by University of Michigan Ross Business School Professors Bob Quinn and Gretchen Spreitzer at the Leaders Connect Breakfast (youtu.be/lOGwHlUBUhA)[2]. I learned that the greatest teachers are those who have the greatest capacity for empathy and are able to recognize and nurture the gifts in their students.

Your Reflections

Reflect and then write a hearty full page about your special gift, including examples from the past and consideration on how to best utilize your gift every day. If you feel you have more than one gift, feel free to do this exercise for each gift you identify.
- Going back to childhood, what have I always been good at?
- What do I do that comes easily for me but it is difficult for others?
- I feel energy and joy when I spend my time doing ____.
- Even if I didn't get paid for it, I would love to get up every day and ____.
- If I could overcome the obstacles in my way, I love to spend my time ____.

---

[2] You may find it easier to find and follow links like this from the resource page for the book on RobPasick.com.

Consider what is the special gift of the important people in your life.

Imagine what you can do to nurture and grow your special gift and the gifts of the important people in your life.

Fill in the blanks: My special gift is ____ and I can use it daily by ____.

In my experience, reflecting on these questions brings clarity.

Your Assignment

Summarize your thoughts on your gift in your Personal Development Plan.

Do You Really Know
What You Do Best?

Years ago, I had trouble reworking my website. I struggled with articulating what I do and how I provide value to my clients. I had lunch with an old friend, Bill Neale, and I sought his advice.

"That's easy," said Bill, "I've known you for a long time, Rob, and you're the very best person I know who helps executives and their teams to solve problems and accelerate improvement in overall business performance." He added, "Not only that, you're also a master at helping people figure out what they want to do next with their careers, and what will make them happy and successful."

"Wow," I said to Bill, "that was so simple...why did I find it so hard when I tried to define it?"

"Because," Bill remarked, "we are often the least likely person to really appreciate what it is we do."

Of course, it should have come as no surprise to me that it was much easier for Bill to identify my strengths than it was for me to do it myself. I should have remembered that people are notoriously bad at self-reporting. The reasons are complex, including: poor self-esteem, our capacity for self-delusion, our tendency to be our own worst enemy, and living in a society where it is much easier to give negative feedback rather than positive.

I invite you to take this opportunity to ask others for feedback on what it is that you do well.

Here are some ideas on how you could go about doing this:

- Take time with friends and family who know you best and ask them what they see as your best qualities and strengths. You might explain that you are doing this as part of a class or coaching assignment.

- Be prepared for some surprising answers. Since we are not that good at self-reflection, you may find that how people describe you is very different than what you expect.

Most of us are familiar with Shakespeare's quote "to thine own self be true." To really know "thine own self," we must have the courage to ask others what they think of us.

CHAPTER THREE
Self-Discovery Step Two:
Uncover Your
Interests and Passions

From a Student

"As a child, I have grown up wanting to be a different person each day. One day, I would want to build a rocket, the next day I dreamt of being a doctor and cure people living in remote areas of India of the deadliest of diseases, the third day I'd want to be a teacher pushing education forward for the under-privileged.

"Looking back, I have realized that the common string connecting all my fantasy professions has always been the urge to help others as much as I can and go beyond looking after myself and my loved ones. Also, being brought up by a single mother I have always been taught to respect everything I have been blessed with (rather) than brooding over what I don't. So for the past few years that has been my mission statement 'to go beyond' in small yet significant ways, just keep pushing beyond myself. Be it volunteering at non-profits focusing on education, taking up leadership roles in organizations that foster innovation, clean-up drives; I have tried to make giving back a lifestyle, rather than something I want to do and I hope to live by this mission at every step in the future as well. My long term as well as short term goals revolve around the same idea. I hope to achieve what I am passionate about through my professional experiences as an electrical engineer."

–Savita Yelamanchili

Discovering Your Passion

"Though, consumed with the hot fire of his purpose, Ahab in all his thoughts and actions ever had in view the ultimate capture of Moby Dick; though he seemed ready to sacrifice all mortal interests to that one passion..."
–Herman Melville, Moby Dick (1851)

A key to becoming a more self-aware is to identify what you are passionate about. The problem is that this search often is a lifetime pursuit. Many people have difficulty identifying their passion. Some find it later in life.

In my work with students, I've come to believe that to discover your passion, begin by identifying your main interests. By knowing what your interests are, you are able to focus your activities, utilize your talents, and make choices which take you closer and closer to discovering your passions.

Most of you have already made important choices in your life. For instance, if you are a business student, you know that, in general, your interests draw you to activities in the business world. If you are reading this as a graduate student, you have decided a career track to pursue.

Your Reflections

Here are some key questions that will enable you to identify your interests and your passions:

What do you stand for?

- What do you care about deeply?
- Is there a societal problem for which you would like to contribute a solution?
- I always tell myself that anything worth achieving requires facing distinct difficulties,

experiencing internal struggle, and accepting big risk. For what goal, are you willing to risk everything? For what are you willing to sacrifice or even suffer to achieve?

What excites you?

Identify your peak moments in life so far. Think of the times when you felt your best, when you felt excited and proud, and when you most felt that time slipped away quickly. When you think of these moments, you are probably recalling moments when your passion was most intense. By discovering what you were doing at those moments, you reveal your passions.

- What did you love to do as a child?
- What did you think you were going to be "when you grew up"?
- What gets you up in the morning?
- What type of conversations engage you?
- What brings you the most joy in life?
- When you have had a great day, what was it you were doing and what are you not doing?
- Passion is about emotion. What topic most evokes a strong emotional reaction in you?
- What do you love to do with your free time?
- What activities give you energy and joy?
- Even if you were not getting paid for it, what occupational activities would you be willing to do for free?
- If you had $1 billion, what would you do?

Create a "**passion masterpiece**" such as a scrapbook or poster. To further discover your passion, begin to clip articles, photos, song lyrics, and images that ignite your spirit. Create a collage full of pictures that excite you. As you begin to build upon your collection, notice to what you are drawn and to what you are indifferent. Add your passion masterpiece (or an image of it or a link to it) to your Personal Development Plan.

Bonus Activity - Ask other people what they think you are passionate about. You might consider talking in person, video chatting, or sending an email to at least three people who know you well to ask them what they see you most passionate about.

What Drains You?

Sometimes you can identify your passions and interests through contemplating their opposites: what drains you of energy?

Here are some prompts to help you draw up a list of areas in in which you are not interested or about which you are not passionate.

- What disciplines or subject did you dislike in school?
- What kinds of tasks and activities do you find you typically put off?
- What are the tasks or activities that leave you very tired at the end of the day?
- What subjects or topics lead you to check out of a conversation or meeting?
- What takes the wind out of your sails?
- What bores you?
- What makes you feel limited or constrained?
- What do you dread?
- What have you quit or been fired from? Why?

Passion Summary Assignment

Unlike for Strengths and Personality, I have found no useful online "passion test" to assign. The way to uncover your passions is to reflect and get feedback from others.

This section contains reflection questions. Now, write a short summary of your passions and interests in your Personal Development Plan.

CHAPTER FOUR
Self-Discovery Step Three:
Understand Your Personality

From a Student

"In particular, I recognize that I am introverted, often preferring to work alone at my desk over asking others for help. I don't need constant interaction to get me through the day, but am sometimes handicapped by my reluctance to socialize. Another blind spot which results from my introversion is my tendency to internalize emotions. Often, when something is wrong, I do not communicate my negative emotions to others, causing a roadblock to my own recovery. This internalization of negative emotion sometimes affects my work, causing me to be less effective at a given task."
–a student

Discover Your Personality

Personality is a characteristic that has been studied extensively by psychologists over the last several decades. Research has defined five aspects of personality. These "big five" are:

- Openness to Experience—do you prefer change to the status quo?
- Conscientiousness (work ethic)—are you organized and disciplined?
- Extraversion—do you enjoy meeting and interacting with new people? Do you recharge yourself socially or alone?
- Agreeableness—are you accommodating or firm?
- Natural Reactions—are you relaxed and calm or excitable/anxious?

These big five personality spectra are often described by their acronym, OCEAN.

Your Reflection

For each of these, where do you feel you are on a range of high–middle–low?

Through relatively quick assessments, it is now possible to understand your personality. Since human beings are notoriously poor at understanding themselves, these personality tests have a severe limitation. They are describing the individual solely based on input from the individual.

In this section, you will take one of these online assessments. Yet, it is also important to include feedback from others.

Your Assignment

> Follow this link to a website where you will be asked to answer 120 questions. You will then receive the PDF of the results of the survey which will enable you to better understand your personality.
> 123test.com/big-five-personality-theory/
> Please fill in your OCEAN test results on your Personal Development Plan.

Consider Your Gender Role

Across the world, children receive different messages about what it means to be a man or a woman. Every culture has its own definition of gender roles and identity. These have as much to do with the culture as they do to biological differences. These days, gender role identity is going through rapid change and is being challenged on many fronts.

In the 1990s I created a table that summarized general gender differences in US culture. I based the right side of the table on research about women from the Stone Center at Wellesley College. The material on the left side, about men, is based on my own observations and the research on the psychology of men in the USA.

Men	Women
Develop independence, self-reliance, autonomy	Develop and maintain relationships
Place importance on following personal dreams, destiny and self-fulfillment	Place importance on connectedness to others
Emphasize learning the rules (what's right or fair)	Emphasize learning empathy skills and relating
In a game, winning counts	In a game, relationships count
Emphasize competition	Emphasize cooperation
Conceal feelings (except anger)	Express feelings (except anger)
Emphasize occupational growth	Emphasize family growth
See a problem and want to fix it	See a problem and want to talk about it

Your Reflection

Look at the table and think about where you stand.

The table represents the stereotypes. We are not all stereotypes. Some of us have more behaviors that are typical of the opposite sex than of our own sex. This is not good or bad. It is just a reality. Gender is a construct, not a biological given.

Review the table and circle the descriptors that best capture your mindset and approach. Once you are through ask yourself these questions:

- Do you fall exactly into either of these gender stereotypes? Where are the areas where you may differ?
- If you are from a different culture, how different are the gender roles in your society? Are they more fluid or more rigid than in the USA?
- If and when you have children, what gender roles do you want to teach them?

Recognize Your Blind Spots

Research shows that often it is not what we see but what we fail to see that causes us to self-destruct. So it is important to become aware of our blind spots.

To drive a car safely, we learn to watch the car's blind spots. The blind spot in a car is a place behind and to the side of a car that the side- and rear-view mirrors don't show well. In Driver's Ed, I was taught to turn my head and check the blind spot before changing lanes. Some cars today have blind spot sensors that alert the driver when there's something there if he uses his turn signal.

You have blind spots just like cars on the road. A blind spot is something others see in us that we do not see in ourselves.

Sometimes our strengths and personality traits come paired with vulnerabilities. Someone who is very empathetic might pay more attention to others than she does to herself, leaving her drained and unable to care for others the way she intends. Or, a very organized person may see the world in too strict a manner to put together ideas from disparate settings. Introverted folks may choose to go it alone in times of stress, yet asking for help could solve their issue more quickly and with less suffering.

Your Reflections

- You can't know your own blind spots. Ask others! Poll people who have known you for a long time and ask them to help you identify your blind spots.
- Be aware of the self-defeating patterns that can be triggered by blind spots. Teach yourself to let go.

- Once you are aware of your blind spots, keep them in mind as you make decisions and interact with others. Ask: Is there any aspect of this where I am giving in to a blind spot?
- Recognize that you will never please everyone all of the time. Don't spend hours worrying about what never will be.
- Give yourself permission to be imperfect.

Your Assignment

Add information on your blind spots to your Personal Development Plan.

CHAPTER FIVE
Self-Discovery Step Four: Manage your Energy and Your Body

From a Student

"As a grad student, I have been overly focused on career-specific goals. I have come to realize that I was happiest as an undergraduate because I was able to balance intellectual stimulation, music, exercise, and friendship. To satisfy my musical interests, I plan to find a jazz band so I can maintain my saxophone skills. ENTR 599 has helped me return to a good exercise routine. My goal for the semester was to complete a half marathon, which I accomplished."
–E.A.

Tips from a 90-Year-Old on Staying Fit in Mind, Body, and Spirit

My mother-in-law, Jean Carino, at age 90+ continues to be strong in mind, body, and spirit. The key to her being able to sustain health and vitality at 90 is that she pays attention to all three of these areas. Her interests include reading, games such as Mah-jongg, and golf. She is an active member of her church. Inspired by her, I have developed these four tips on how to stay strong in mind, body, and spirit throughout your life.

Four Tips on How to **Stay Strong in Mind, Body, and Spirit**

1. Take an honest inventory.
2. Make regular habits and rituals to stay fit.
3. Be mindful in all that you do.
4. Practice love.

First, on a regular basis, take an honest inventory and give yourself a grade on how well you are doing in taking care of yourself on:

- Mind (0-10 scale, 10 excellent)
- Body (0-10 scale, 10 excellent)
- Spirit (0-10 scale, 10 excellent)

Second, create regular habits or rituals to be sure to do something daily to stay fit in all three areas. Some examples are:

- Journal—writing and/or drawing
- Meditate, pray
- Spend time outdoors, enjoy nature
- Engage in a creative activity
- Exercise
- Participate in sports
- Play, including games with friends and family
- Engage in stimulating conversations
- Read meaningful literature

Third, be mindful in all that you do.
- Do one thing at a time
- Be aware of the impact you have on others
- Do good for others without seeking benefit for yourself

Fourth, practice love.
- Look for specific ways to love yourself
- Love your family and friends; this may take some creativity when they are far away from you.
- Love the world you live in and protect the earth

Your Assignment

> Imagine you've reached 90, and you are looking back on your secret sauce for having had a successful life. What ingredients would have gone into your secret sauce for health in mind, body, and spirit? Describe them in a letter to yourself. For example, "Dear Rob, this is your 90-year-old-self writing you a letter..." Date the letter and revisit it over the years.

Body and Body Image

For most young people, body and body image are primary concerns and are often the source deep anxiety. A major part of self-awareness is to develop an accurate sense of how you feel about your body.

Some students have body image challenges such as eating disorders and self-loathing about their bodies. Since every college campus has resources for students, please seek resources early to best take care of yourself and your friends.

Your Reflections

- List the positive qualities that make your body unique to you.
- What do you do each day/week/month to care for your physical body?
- How do others support you and how do you engage with others to eat and drink healthfully?
- How do others support you in health?
- How do you engage with others to participate in healthy activities?
- What positive changes could you make in the next week/month toward better self-care?
- What resources are available to you if you or a friend are having thoughts or actions of an unhealthy lifestyle?
- Who would support you to work toward a more positive self-image?

Your Assignment

Write a paragraph summarizing what you do well to care for your body. Write a second paragraph outlining any plans you have to improve your self-care.

From a Student

"A meal is never satisfactory unless it has the right balance of sugar and spice, the best basketball teams are most successful when they have both a good defense and a good offense. I believe that the key to making the most out of something is to find the right balance.

"As a high school student, I was crazy about sports, be it playing them, or watching them. I realize that I was happy and could work to my fullest potential because of the balance I found between sports and education.

"Being able to devote time to both of these realms allowed me to keep myself both mentally and physically refreshed. I have noticed that as I have grown older and progressed from high school to college, the challenge of being able to find this balance evolves and changes with time."

–Rohan Tirumale

Manage Your Energy as Well as Your Time

Have you ever heard people say, "I don't have enough time?" Business owner Mary Martin, of Holland, Michigan, interprets this as people not having enough energy.

When I hear about low energy from a client, I first ask whether my clients feel engaged in their work. Then I ask about any family or health issues that may be preoccupying them. If there are some, I find out if there is any action they can take to resolve these issues. I also ask whether they are getting enough sleep and enough exercise.

Juan greatly improved his energy by taking a 20-minute walk/run with his dog every morning. Irene switched to a four-day workweek to be able to spend more time with her two young children. William sought a family therapist to help with problems with his son, who has attention deficit disorder. Alfred began taking his children to the golf course every Sunday for an outing. Josh went to a sleep disorder clinic to find out why his sleep was constantly disrupted.

These kinds of actions helped these leaders avoid the burnout that so often accompanies people in demanding roles. When you're a leader, you don't have to prove yourself with a superhuman effort or superhuman time commitment. Sustainability is more important. And to achieve that, you have to know what re-energizes you. It's all about discipline and knowing what recharges your batteries.

Managing time often is really about managing energy. It's not just becoming more efficient. People often will try to do two things at once—take calls in the car while driving home, for instance. But if the person previously used the drive home to unwind and recharge, now they're not giving themselves time for that. They're still working.

Time is a finite resource. You really can't cheat time.

Your Reflections

- If you don't know what re-energizes you, ask the people around you. Ask your mate what he or she notices about your behavior—when you're up or down—and what led to it.
- Keep an energy journal so you can zero in on when you lose your energy and when it's at a peak. Write in the journal the time of day, type of activities, and people (or solitude) that correlate with your high-energy moments. Accept that you need these stimuli to boost your energy.
- Ask yourself what might be draining your energy. Are you fully engaged in your work? Are there family or health problems that are preoccupying you? Are you getting enough sleep? Enough exercise?
- Take a nap.
- Spend time on activities that give you a full sense of purpose.
- Meditate.
- Go to places that energize you, not to ones that drain your energy. (I write this as I sit in my local cupcake shop with many happy customers.)

Your Assignment

Take the free online energy profile from the Human Performance Institute. This a self-assessment measures your physical, emotional, mental, and spiritual energy to improve your performance. performanceprograms.com/self-assessments/personal-development/energy-profile/

How you allocate your time exercise.

First, draw a pie chart showing where you want your time to be going each day.

Then, over the next week, try to create daily pie charts of how you actually spend your time. Compare the two and create an alignment a plan. (See the Chapter on Goal Setting for more support on how to do this.)

CHAPTER SIX
Self-Discovery Step Five: Care for Your Mind

A Poem: No Prozac for You

Lucy you hang your head whenever you've done wrong, yet

You rebound from your guilt at the first friendly gesture.

A "good girl" is all you need to revive your spirit.

No Prozac for you, Lu.

After a few minutes with your head buried in your pillow you're like a new dog, ready to roll over and play again.

–Robert Pasick, Ph.D in Conversations with My Old Dog

Is Your Thinking Making You Miserable?

When I first moved to New York City in 1968, after graduating from the University of Michigan, I was alone. Unless I could find a teaching job I was going to be drafted into the Vietnam War. It didn't take me long to realize I was becoming depressed and anxious.

Having been a psychology major, I knew psychotherapy could help, but I could not afford it. In college I had admired the work of Psychologist Albert Ellis, and his development of Rational Emotive Therapy. I checked out his Institute for Rational Living, and found out that Ellis demonstrated his therapy on volunteers in front of a live audience. I was so impressed by Ellis' work that I joined one of his Saturday therapy groups.

I have to say I was transformed by the experience. I learned that it was not any specific situation that made a person anxious, but how the person interpreted that situation. I realized that rather than focusing on the sunny side of life, I had been taught to be very cautious and pessimistic about life. The experience of therapy was a key element in my decision to go to graduate school in psychology at Harvard.

Today, almost fifty years later, I still practice Rational Emotive Therapy (today this is more familiarly known as Cognitive Behavioral Therapy). This method teaches people to recognize faulty, irrational thinking and to replace it with a more rational, cognitively based approach to life. It has been the cornerstone of my personal and professional approach. I utilize it with all of my coaching and clinical clients.

Here are some of the core concepts of Cognitive Behavioral Therapy that you can use in your daily life.

- Recognize when you are making yourself upset by clinging to irrational and faulty thinking.
- Strive to understand HOW others are thinking about situations before you judge them.
- When you are troubled, get past any stigma that you have that therapy is a sign of weakness. Rather, reinterpret your thinking to see therapy as a sign of strength and courage.
- Recognize that there are three musts that hold us back: I must do well, you must treat me well, the world must be easy and fair.
- Stop 'shoulding' on yourself (e.g. telling yourself you *should* be loved and approved of by everyone for everything you do).

Today there are online approaches to help people manage their anxiety and depression. Here is an excellent article from The Atlantic describing these services: theatlantic.com/health/archive/2015/05/the-startup-that-wants-to-end-social-anxiety/392900/

Challenge Your Irrational Ideas

Many of life's problems stem not so much from the things that happen to us as from how we interpret these events. Whether we realize it or not, most of us carry around one or more irrational ideas that act as filters for our experiences. These may cause us to react more strongly and inappropriately to events than is warranted.

In his research, psychologist Albert Ellis identified a famous "dirty dozen" of these irrational ideas. See if you recognize yourself in any of them:

1. Adults must be loved by significant others for almost everything they do.
2. Certain acts are awful or wicked, and the people who perform them should be damned.
3. It's horrible when things are not the way we like them to be.
4. Human misery is invariably externally caused and forced on us by outside people and events.
5. If something is or may be dangerous or fearsome, we should be terribly upset and obsess about it endlessly.
6. It's easier to avoid than to face life's difficulties and responsibilities.
7. We absolutely need something or someone stronger or greater than ourselves on which to rely.
8. We should be thoroughly competent, intelligent and achieving in all possible respects.
9. Because something once strongly affected our life, it should indefinitely affect it.
10. We must have certain and perfect control over things.

11. Human happiness can be achieved by inertia and inaction.

12. We have virtually no control over our emotions and cannot help feeling disturbed about things.

Once you learn to recognize your irrational baggage, you can challenge those assumptions as they arise—and close the lid on them.

Your Assignment

Which of the twelve irrational ideas do you recognize? Circle your top three. Reflect on ways in which these three might interfere with your health and success. Be vigilant on how they may interfere with your thinking. Develop a plan for learning to challenge these thoughts.

Add your top three irrational beliefs to the Personal Development Plan. Describe your plan to counteract these beliefs.

Get the Help You Need

We often don't hesitate to seek expert advice when we're trying to learn a skill like golf or cooking. Sometimes we seek out other experts— therapists or coaches—when something feels broken. But sometimes we don't seek help at all because we are fearful or have feelings of shame.

Every semester, students share privately with me that they have a health concern, yet most are reluctant to talk about it in the classroom because they are ashamed or embarrassed. Health concerns for students include:

- psychological disorders including those involving attention, anxiety, depression, drugs, alcohol, or stress;
- physical disorders including bowel and blood diseases.

While some students have these issues, many other students are affected by struggles of close friends and family members.

Your Reflections

- If you think you have a psychiatric problem, seek therapy.
- If you have a health problem, go to a doctor.
- If you're having trouble managing your work role, go to a coach.
- If you've got an addiction, go to a 12-step meeting or consult your physician.
- If there's trouble on the home front, go to a family therapist or marriage counselor.
- If you're having a spiritual crisis, seek out a clergy person.
- If you're not sure what you should do, consult a friend or someone close to you.

- Pray for guidance and remember the adage, "God helps those who help themselves."

Your Assignment

Consider what you need and why you hold back from giving to yourself. Usually it is something like fear of finding out something you don't want to know or cost in addressing a problem.

If there is something that's holding you back, it won't go away on its own. Make a plan for addressing the issue. Who will you ask for help? By when? How will you do it?

How to Start Meditating

For a variety of reasons, I often suggest to my clients that they learn to meditate and develop a practice of mindfulness. I have found that through meditation, one learns to focus attention, control negative thoughts, and achieve peacefulness.

Often, my clients are overwhelmed with how difficult they believe meditation can be. As a way to get started, I offer them a simple method that I learned years ago from the book *How to Meditate* by Eknath Easwaran. By devoting just thirty minutes a day, they learn how to successfully maintain a meditation and mindfulness practice.

Thirty minutes a day is a lot in the beginning. You can build up to it with a smaller time commitment.

Five Steps to Get Started Meditating

1. Find a passage of literature which you find inspirational. This could be a poem, a prayer, a song lyric, etc. Spend 10 minutes reading the passage.
2. Memorize a portion of this passage
3. With your passage in mind, sit in a calm space with your eyes closed for 10 minutes.
4. While focusing on your breathing, on each exhale breath repeat one word of your passage. For example: If your passage is the "Serenity Prayer", with your first breath you would say "God," followed by the second breath, "grant", the third "me" ...etc., and continue until you have completed the passage. If you lose your concentration or place, start over from beginning of the sentence you were on.

5. After your 10 minutes of meditation, write reflectively in a journal for another 10 minutes. The only rule is to write something, whether it is a few words or several pages.

An Alternative

You can use a meditation timer app on your phone to guide and support your practice. Once you commit to meditating for a certain time, you can set the app to play a gentle sound at the end of the time. The app can also log your meditation (date, time, duration).

Sophisticated apps can remind you to meditate, turn off the sound and notifications on your device when you meditate, play soothing sounds to help you drown out nearby distractions, give you access to guided meditation sessions, and connect you with others who meditate at the same time. Insight Timer (free, available for iPhone and Android phones) is a great app to explore.

Give it a Try!

Since many of my clients are working at a rapid pace and multitasking much of the time, I recommend this practice as a way to slow down and regain control of their mind. Personally, it is not something I am rigid about, but I know I am at my best when I start my day with this routine.

Practice Self-Reflection

Meditation is only one of the ways to practice self-reflection. You may prefer to do it in connection with your faith. You may want to keep a journal. Or you may prefer talking with someone on a regular basis—your significant other, a friend or even another couple. Sometimes it's easier to be open and reflective with those who aren't part of your immediate family.

My wife and I see our longtime friends, Barry and Eileen, a few times a year, and we've developed a ritual as part of our get-togethers. We generally have dinner, and then everyone takes a turn, talking about what has happened in the intervening time and whatever else is on the person's mind. It is self-reflection, practiced within a group.

This has been very helpful over the years as we go through life's ups and downs. It's not all serious talk, either. We laugh a lot as well. Barry and Eileen have become part of our extended family.

Your Reflections

- Set aside time for reflection.
- Find an activity—meditation, yoga, writing, prayer, conversation—that allows you to express your inner life.
- Keep a journal.
- Find an aid, perhaps a book, a class, or an online site, to help you and give you encouragement.
- Turn to a 12-step program if you need help with an addiction.
- Take advantage of faith-based spiritual retreats and study groups.
- Talk to a therapist if you need special help.
- Use your drive time for reflection.

Delayed Grief over Grandpa Izzie

Grief is an emotional reaction to loss. It is what we feel when we lose someone, something, or even a goal. Grief is the process we go through in the aftermath of that loss. Our problem is that our grief is often short-circuited. We have not been allowed, or do not allow ourselves, adequate time to grieve over our losses. Beginning with boyhood and continuing throughout the life cycle, we are told that the appropriate way to handle loss of any kind is to acknowledge it stoically then to get on with life, quickly, which usually means acting like the loss never occurred.

This simply does not work. If a loss is not adequately mourned, it can have adverse effects on a person's psychological development, particularly on the way the person behaves in future relationships.

A few years ago, I became aware of the consequences of not having mourned the loss of my maternal grandfather, who committed suicide in 1970 when I was twenty-three. Here's the story of what reignited the grief so many years later.

After having put off cleaning the garage for months, I decided to confront the tangled extension cords, the dust-covered garden tools, and the boxes filled with items long forgotten and not missed but somehow too important to be thrown away.

Reluctantly, I dug in. Not far into the sorting and tossing, I paused to examine the contents of a gray metal box. I was unprepared for my reaction as I discovered an old electric sander with a manila tag on it. I recognized it immediately as a pawn ticket from the shop where my grandfather had worked most of his life. In his beautiful handwriting I could still make out the words, "Henry Washington, June, 1958," the name of the man who had hocked the sander and the date it had to be claimed. Evidently Mr. Washington had not claimed it on time, so my grandfather had bought it cut-rate. Gazing at that ticket, I realized I had not seen anything in my grandfather's handwriting since his death in 1970.

I remembered myself, as a child, living with my parents and grandparents in a small suburban home, eagerly awaiting the return of Grandpa Izzie from the pawnshop on Saturday night. He would often bring home an array of drills, radios, and other unclaimed items. I always thought of them as his special gifts to me. Holding that ticket, I felt the rush of memories it summoned. It occurred to me that the small piece of cardboard was the only memento I still had of Izzie.

During the Detroit riots of 1967, the pawnshop was burned down. Less dramatically but just as inevitably, Izzie, out of work for the first time in his life, began deteriorating, too. For income, he rekindled his old habit of gambling; as the losses mounted, his drinking increased. He began issuing suicide threats. I was teaching school in New York City when I received the call from my father. Izzie's final threat was not idle. He had killed himself by swallowing jeweler's acid, just as he had threatened many times before.

As I showed my wife and kids that tag, I felt myself fighting back the tears. In a way I wished they would finally flow. Due to the mixed feelings associated with his suicide, I had never been able to cry over the loss of my grandfather. The situation was made more complicated by the family's decision to keep the cause of death a secret. At his age, we figured why dishonor his memory? No one would doubt the family story that this heavy smoker had had a heart attack. Little did I understand that keeping the suicide a secret would block me from adequately mourning the grandfather I had loved so dearly. My friends knew my grandfather had died, but out of loyalty to my family I could share with no one my anguish over the manner of his death.

In the years immediately following his death, my feelings about Izzie alternated between guilt and anger. As an only child growing up in a house of adults, my specialty had been to keep everyone cheerful, especially this alternately morose and exuberant man. I had failed to cheer him up this time. It seemed perfectly natural for me to major in psychology in college. As a psych student, moreover, shouldn't I have recognized the warning signs of suicide and been able to prevent it? Maybe if I hadn't left home he wouldn't have become so depressed. Maybe I should have invited him to visit me in New York City. The list of shoulds and maybes was long and persistent whenever I was reminded of Izzie, which happened often since I like to listen to Detroit Tiger baseball on the radio. Izzie always seemed to have a portable radio stuck in his ear, listening to Ernie Harwell, the voice of the Tigers. (Izzie liked to call them the Pussycats in those days of constant fifth-place finishes.)

The only match for my guilt was my anger. Somehow I could not easily forgive him for having tarnished two of my life's greatest joys. Izzie had always been my number one fan. How often I had heard him say, "Robbie, you're going to be a great man someday." With his encouragement I had made two important decisions in 1970: to apply to graduate school and to ask my girlfriend, Pat, to marry me. How sad and disappointed I felt that he had not waited around to hear about my acceptance at Harvard and to attend our wedding. If he had really cared about me, he would not have taken his life just four months before the wedding.

As the years went by, though, sorrow emerged as the dominant emotion. I missed him. I ached at the memory of him waking me up in the morning by imitating an alarm clock or driving me and my friends to high school in his '61 Chevy Nova. "Who's kicking me in the amplifier?" he'd ask the laughing teenagers in the backseat.

I was sad, too, that my own sons never had a chance to meet Izzie. They would have enjoyed this slight, handsome man who made bad jokes, spoke his own foreign tongue especially designed for his grandchildren, and who would pile all the kids in the neighborhood into his small car to take us to an afternoon Tigers game.

As I showed my sons the ticket, I was pleased that they, too, have had wonderful relationships with their own grandfathers. I know, of course, that they were in no way responsible for their grandfathers' well-being. This thought helped me to realize that I wasn't to blame, and Izzie wasn't to be punished for taking his own life. Now I can understand how painful his undiagnosed manic-depression must have been. No, the most painful facet of Izzie's death — missing him — was simply a function of his passing away. Suicide and heart attacks have equal status there.

I detached the tag and gently cleaned off the dust. I realized that maybe a pawn ticket may be an appropriate memory for this man. In some ways he had pawned his own life away. But in many ways, I owe a debt to him as well. He contributed much to who I am today: to the development of my playful side; to my courage to take risks; and to my love of baseball. Now I am determined not to allow his manner of death to obliterate the spirit of the man. To me he had been a hero, a dapper guy in a Fedora and a natty sport coat with his shoes always shined. As I placed the ticket in my wallet, I vowed never to stow it or his memory away again.

Your Assignment

> Grief occurs not only over death. Grief can be a reaction to almost any type of loss, and we have all experienced many. I invite you to reflect on your own losses and to ask yourself how adequately you have mourned these losses.

CHAPTER SEVEN
Self-Discovery Step Six: Invest in Your Relationships

From a Student

"Managing Professional Relationships class has benefited me greatly. I have successfully moved across the country to Seattle, WA. The class gave me confidence in my abilities to use my network throughout this new journey, and I have managed to make a lot of new connections along the way.

"I work in Sales for Microsoft, so everything I do is based on the professional relationships I have built. I had my first official review with my manager and he highlighted how impressed he was with my abilities to connect with both the customer and the team I work alongside. As soon as I was given this feedback, my mind took me back to class where we sat in a circle setting goals and learning from professionals who had successfully established themselves in diverse industries. There is no doubt in my mind that everyone who takes the class leaves a better person who is well equipped for success in their personal and professional life."

–Cassandra Webb

The Harvard Study of Adult Development

The Harvard Study of Adult Development may be the longest study of adult life that's ever been done. For 75 years, they've tracked the lives of 724 men, year after year, asking about their work, their home lives, their health, and of course asking all along the way without knowing how their life stories were going to turn out. The clearest message that we get from this 75-year study is this: **Good relationships keep us happier and healthier**. Period.

Throughout my 40-year career as a psychologist, **I believe most strongly that the cornerstone of good relationships is self-awareness**.

Here's the link to a TED talk on the Harvard Study of Adult Development. ted.com/talks/robert_waldinger_what_makes_a_good_life_lessons_from_the_longest_study_on_happiness

Your Reflection

What is your major takeaway from the TED talk?

When Oprah Calls

When my kids were teenagers in the early 1990s, I got really caught up in writing books about men. I'd published two books, *Men in Therapy* and *Awakening from the Deep Sleep,* about men and their relationships and how they should live their lives differently. As the books were very well received, I quickly followed with another book, *What Every Man Needs to Know.*

As I began to experience a fair degree of success, I started to act as though my time as an author and thought leader was more important than my time as a father and husband. I became obsessed with traveling, giving workshops, and contemplating what my next book was going to be.

One spring, we scheduled a long-overdue family vacation on Hilton Head Island. My cousins from Texas joined us, too. Only three days into the week-long trip, my assistant in Ann Arbor called to say, "You got a call from a producer on the Oprah show. They have an opening on the show and they want you to be on it." But the opening was just two days away—in the middle of our vacation.

Without hesitating or consulting my family, I made arrangements to fly to Chicago. Later, I told my wife and kids how excited I was. They were gracious about my leaving, even helping me buy a new suit to wear on the show, but I didn't think about the fact that I was leaving them and my cousins.

It wasn't until I returned a few days later to a rather icy reception that it dawned on me: I had been so caught up in my success that I had put my own need for fame ahead of the family's need for togetherness and time with Dad.

I'd done a lot of things in my life, but the fact that I was on The Oprah Winfrey Show was special. Later, my friends started calling me "Oprah Man" and asking me what Oprah was like. I'm not ashamed to admit that it went straight to my head. I had become seduced by success. It was amazing how easy it was for me to set aside some of my basic values. And the irony of it, of course, was that my book was about how men should shed their self-centered behavior. I found myself becoming a case study for my own book!

It took a while, but eventually I came to my senses. Being a good dad and good husband were more important than being on Oprah. It was time for me to back off and reset my priorities.

Cultivate Friendships

Despite my professional training, I've had difficulty expressing myself to friends. I tend to hide behind my therapist's mask. So, when an old friend, Nick, once chewed me out for being so silent while he had no problem talking about himself, I had to agree—and I thanked him for his honesty. He got me to work on this issue.

Men often have a challenging time cultivating friendships, yet reconnecting with old friends and making and maintaining new ones is essential to our growth and development. Friends are vital to health and happiness; they can even help reduce stress.

Studies have shown that people who have intimate relationships are more likely to survive heart attacks and less likely to develop cancer and serious infections. There also is a strong correlation between a lack of social relationships and high blood pressure, smoking and obesity.

Without close friends, we battle loneliness and feel disconnected from the past. We often pine for the sense of connectedness we had as kids. Lots of things get in the way of maintaining friendships, including the competitive nature of our society. But we should try diligently to resist these pressures.

Your Reflections

- Come to terms with your relationship with your parents, because these ties are the prototypes for your relationships with peers.
- Reconnect with old friends and set up social gatherings with them.
- Go to reunions.
- Look for ways to open up to current friends: Plan a trip or outing. Talk about something you usually might not be inclined to bring up.

- Identify the obstacles that tend to get in the way of your friendships: fear of rejection, unresolved conflicts, insufficient time, competitiveness, past failures.
- Recognize that friendships aren't just about "being liked"; they're also about taking care of yourself by feeling connected to others.
- Call at least one friend a week.
- Do something—join a group, take a class, learn a new hobby or become a volunteer— that will put you in contact with others.
- Don't create a situation where all of your friendships are tied to work or groups you belong to.
- Be open and honest about yourself.
- Make couple friendships and set up times to spend with couples you and your mate both like.

Your Assignment

> Reconnect with an old friend with whom you've fallen out of contact.
>
> Arrange a lunch or outing with a classmate or colleague you do not yet know well.

Forget Trying to Control People

Leaders worry themselves to death over how to get people to do what they want them to do. My book *Conversations with My Old Dog* is a series of poems about the "talks" I used to have with my aging yellow lab Lucy. The poem "Control" includes these lines:

We people spend much of our time on the illusion of control—
we order our lives and try
to order the lives of others.
However, we learn—as with our dogs—
that we may get folks to sit
but never to stay.

I offer the same advice to the people I coach. It's difficult enough to control your own behavior; it's a losing proposition to try to control others'. Learn to appreciate their behavior instead.

Your Reflections

- No matter what your title, treat everyone with respect.
- Take the time to engage people; ask questions and let them ask you questions. Give honest answers. Listen to their responses. It's better when you can hear from others what they think should be done. Collectively, you can try to control the outcomes.
- Be willing to accept the mood and behavior swings of others. They, like you, are human.
- Don't overestimate how well you know even the people closest to you—your spouse, your children, your parents. No matter how familiar you are with them, you cannot control them. Learn to enjoy the surprises

rather than treating them as a sign of irrationality or rebellion.

- Keep in mind that groups are even more complex than individuals. Appreciate the good things that can emerge when everyone feels empowered to speak.
- Give yourself a pat on the back or make a note of the times when you manage to treat the behavior of others in a more positive way than you once would have.
- Work at controlling the things you can control: eat healthfully, exercise regularly and seek sources of inspiration to boost your emotional well-being.
- At best, you can only control one person: yourself.

Your Assignment

Consider - are you someone who tries to control people? If so, is this something you want to change about yourself? Write out your plan for change.

Consider - are you someone who is afraid to stand up for yourself? If so, is this something you want to change about yourself? Write out your plan for change.

In your plan for change, describe why you need to change, what you plan to change, by when, from whom you need support, and how you will do it.

The Importance of Connections

From a student:

"In this past month, I was lucky to have a chance to visit LA for a conference, and using this opportunity, I visited several of the contacts I've had for years online and finally met up with them in person. The courage to ask them for a meet up and the confidence to keep our conversation flowing during a meal were vital skills I learned from the class, and I could feel that they worked out really well. Even though those contacts haven't got me any actual jobs yet...it felt great to just make new friends, hearing their stories in life in general and hearing stories about the industry through their lens seemed more precious than simply having a contact who can give me a job. Because at the end of the day, it really is the people who make our lives extraordinary rather than the job itself, and networking can be so much fun if we turn our focus on hearing people's stories instead of job seeking. That's the biggest thing I learned from this class, and as a recent-grad who's still figuring out what to do with my life, I appreciate this skill and the mindset a lot."
–N.H.

Recently, I have helped several people make job changes. In all cases, they had one thing in common. **They were able to leverage their connections to secure the new job**. This is no surprise to me. I so strongly believe in the importance of connection that when I created my business years ago, I called it "**Leaders *Connect*.**" Additionally, each month I hold a networking event, called Leaders Connect Breakfast. Each breakfast meeting starts with an activity to promote networking. Each participant has an opportunity to introduce him or herself, and to say what it is they may need or are offering.

As an example of this process, check out Part 1 of this video from a Leaders Connect event: youtu.be/YeXJRR2f_6Y

Here are my 10 key do's and don'ts for being successfully connected to others:

1. **DO** help those with whom you are connected.
2. **DO NOT** expect reciprocity on a one to one basis. Help others without expecting that they will help you in return.
3. **DO** build your network by joining and actively participating in community and workplace groups. The key word here is ACTIVELY.
4. **DO NOT** just show up. To be well connected you have to volunteer, do some work, and give back to the organization.
5. **DO** seek to be connected to a diverse group of individuals from different spheres of society and different types of work.
6. **DO NOT** hang out and only connect with people who are only like yourself.
7. **DO** actively relate to others when you go to events. The best way to relate is to show interest in the other person by asking meaningful questions. If you are shy or introverted, make a plan ahead of time with conversation starters and a few details to share about yourself.
8. **DO NOT** only talk about yourself. An elevator speech is fine, but it is more powerful to show interest in the other people at the event.
9. **DO** keep in touch with your friends, family, and colleagues on a regular basis.
10. **DO NOT** rely on email to stay connected. Set up times for coffee, drinks, or lunch, hang out

at places where you are likely to run into your network, and pick up the phone.

Remember, at every level of life, the living world works through cooperation. We are all interconnected and interdependent.

Checklist to Grow Connections

- Ask like-minded individuals to **get together** for coffee, lunch, or a drink *(at least weekly)*.
- Go to **networking** meetings *(at least twice a month)*.
- Work in a public place such as the coffee shop where you are **likely to run into people** with whom you could share ideas (and of course strike up conversations with these people).
- **Post your ideas** or links to good articles on LinkedIn, Facebook or your blog *(at least weekly)*.
- **Send interesting articles** to people who might also find them interesting *(at least weekly)*.
- **Respond** with more than "I like" to other people's posts *(daily or several times a week)*. For example, you can respond with a question.
- Join a *monthly* **round table**.
- Ask others to **give you endorsements** directly or on LinkedIn (I always appreciate your endorsements).

Your Assignment

Do an honest assessment of how well you are able to network (on a scale of 0-10 with 10 being excellent).

Consider what you do well and what you want to do better.

Create a plan for improving your networking skills. In your plan, detail why you need to improve, what you will improve, how you will do this, by when, and from whom you need support.

Fill those Buckets

Authors Tom Rath and Donald O. Clifton used research by the Gallup Organization to craft the bestseller *How Full Is Your Bucket?*

Their basic theory is that we start out every day with a bucket that is emptied or filled by what others say and do to us. We each also have a dipper. We can use it to fill other people's buckets by delivering positive messages or we can dip from others' buckets by delivering negative messages. When we fill others' buckets, we replenish our own. And when we take from others' buckets, we deplete our own.

The process is contagious. If you fill others' buckets with positive messages, they will carry it forward. So, if you work with me and I build you up, you're more likely to build up the people you come in contact with. If I drain your bucket, you're more likely to dump on others.

Marvin rose through the ranks to lead a unit of his company. He was extremely popular in part because he was so positive with people. He saw his ability to encourage people as a major focus of his life. He made it his mission. He wasn't afraid to confront people when necessary, but he tried to be more positive than negative.

When there was an opening to move higher in the organization, Marvin was one of many candidates considered. In the end, he got the job in part because of the trail of good feelings he had left behind him. Don't misunderstand—Marvin wasn't a flatterer. His weren't empty gestures. He sincerely tried to see the best in everyone, all the time.

- Keep track of the abundances of your day— the times when someone has been nice to you or when you've done someone a favor, when a meeting has gone particularly well or when you've offered someone praise or encouragement. Jot them down on paper or on your device. People remember and respect those who make them feel special. You really have only three choices when you respond to others: praise, ignore or criticize.
- Turn a negative into a positive. If you notice someone seems out of sorts or is struggling, ask what's wrong. Find out what kind of help they need or whether they have the resources to get the job done.
- Be genuine about your praise. Don't manufacture it for the sake of appearances.
- Keep in mind research by psychologist John Gottman that shows healthy relationships have a ratio of five positive interactions for every negative one. So if you're handing out more corrections than pats on the back, people are going to start feeling bad about themselves.
- Be specific about what you praise. Highlight a report the person submitted or a comment they made in a meeting.
- Keep track of your own daily achievements, however small.
- Remember: Nine out of 10 people say they're more productive when they're around positive people.
- Fill another's bucket and you automatically fill your own.
- Smile. Nothing gives as much happiness as the gift of awareness.

Your Assignment

Read the student quote below. For the next week, keep track of how well you fill the buckets of those around you. No matter how good you are at being positive with other people, there's almost always room for improvement. Create a plan for yourself how you will become better at filling other people's buckets in the future.

"One activity that stayed with me was when we went around the room and had to compliment each other. It is such a simple task in principle but was actually rather difficult to think of compliments on the spot for people that I had only known for a few weeks. I find that it is easy to notice when someone does something wrong, and it is easy to tell that person that they messed up. However, unless I am on the lookout for the things I like about others, many positives go unnoticed and upraised. Since that activity I have tried to more actively look for the positives of people around me, and when I see them, to let those people know. Everyone likes a sincere compliment so why shouldn't we give them out more?"
–Jeffrey Plott

Apologize When You're Wrong

One year on vacation, when my wife and I were preparing for a doubles tennis match against our sons, I came out to the court after the boys to warm up. I asked Adam, who was 15 at the time, to move to the other end of the court, so I could hit to him and 11-year-old Daniel. But Adam balked. "Why don't you hit with Dan on your end, and I'll stay here on my end?" he said. That ticked me off, and when Dan sided with Adam, it ticked me off some more.

Though Adam reluctantly trudged to the other end, I was still irritated as I hit the first practice shot to him. He swung so hard that the ball flew right past me, close to my head. That did it. I threw down my racket, yelled some more and stomped off the court.

Adam did come and apologize a few minutes later, but he also complained about my rudeness. We played the set—which they won, of course—but later, after I'd had time to reflect, I also apologized to Adam.

"Dad," he said, "that's the first time I ever remember winning an argument with you."

I was startled by that, because I prided myself on being a fair and understanding dad.

"Yeah," Adam said, "but this is the first time you've admitted you were wrong without giving me a lecture about what I had done wrong."

Your Reflections

- Love does not mean never having to say you're sorry or wrong about something.
- Leaders aren't more perfect than other people. Be strong enough to admit a mistake and set the record straight.

- Don't try to hide your areas of vulnerability. Everyone has them.
- Recognize when you are being domineering.
- Talk it out with someone you have been upset with—the sooner, the better.
- Learn to apologize without adding blame. An example of what not to say is "I apologize ... but you provoked me."

Your Assignment

Keep track for a week of how often you apologize, and whether you are successful at apologizing without blaming the other person.

One thing I notice is that women often over-apologize. Think about whether this fits for you and how you will change this. Especially watch over your use of the word "sorry."

Learn People's Stories

Oral historian Alan Lomax once said, "The essence of America is not within the headline heroes ... but in the everyday folks who live and die unknown, yet leave their dreams as legacies."

Everyone has a story, and if you take the time to discover them, you will forge strong bonds. Ask simple questions, such as "Where'd you grow up?" "How many people are in your family?" Pay attention to little things.

When meeting a new client, I make it a point to look around the person's office. One time, I saw a Detroit Tigers pennant poster from the 1930s. I'm a Tigers fan, so I asked about it. That led to a discussion of how the man found the poster when his wife took him to an antiques show. And then I noticed a newspaper article about a boy with Down syndrome. So I asked whether it was the man's son, and he said yes. I told him I'd worked with Down cases and had done my dissertation on this. And so we spent half an hour talking about his son and his achievements. We had an instant bond.

David Meitz, who was a manager at Reuters at the time of the September 11 terrorist attacks, lost colleagues in the collapse of the World Trade Center. Even though he supervised about 100 people, he was deeply troubled by the fact that he could not come up with a mental picture of one of his missing team members. Meitz, now chief technology officer for Investment Technology Group Inc., vowed that he wouldn't let it happen again and that he would always get to know the stories and the faces of those who report to him.

Your Reflections

- Ask people about their lives—and listen to their answers. "If you take the time to listen, you'll find wisdom, wonder and poetry in their lives," writes David Isay in *Listening Is an Act of Love*.
- Ask family members about their day. Listen especially closely to your children when they respond. Their stories are never mundane to them.
- Ask people about the family pictures they have on their desks.
- People generally love recounting tales from the past. Get them to open up with simple questions about their families and where they once lived or went to school.
- Look around. Notice what people are wearing or what's in their office. What you see is a jumping off point for a conversation.
- Learn to ask the kinds of questions that get people talking about themselves.
- Tell your own stories, including those of people who helped you get where you are today.
- Keep in mind these words from Gabriel Garcia Marquez:

"What matters most in life is not what happens to you, but what you remember and how you remember it."

Your Assignment

Visit either StoryCorps.org or StoriesforHope.org.

StoryCorps' mission is to "preserve and share humanity's stories in order to build connections between people and create a more just and compassionate world." Listen at StoryCorps.org

Stories for Hope's mission is to "heal through the Rwandan tradition of intergenerational storytelling." Pat Pasick, Ph.D., was honored as a 2014 Purpose Prize Fellow for this project. Listen on StoriesforHope.org Many of the stories are recorded in Kinyarwanda, and there's always an English transcript you can read.

Listen to a few stories on one of these sites. Then interview a trusted family member for comments on the thesis of this class: professional success is a function of your ability to manage relationships well.

Write up your interview in (3-5 paragraphs). Please feel free to respond to any or all of the following prompts, or discuss another aspect of this exercise that was meaningful to you.

Discuss why you choose to interview this person.

What were your key questions going into the interview?

Did the interview go as you expected? Explain.

Write one or two meaningful takeaways from this interview/exercise.

What piece of insight or advice did you receive that you think is worth passing on to a friend?

Avoid Cutoffs

When people have a relationship that has become too difficult, they may be tempted to cut off the other person cold. You see this in the work setting as well as in families. It's very damaging to the person on the receiving end because they have no way to try to fix the relationship. And it's also damaging to the person who resorts to this tactic because they invariably cut themselves off from more and more people and become ever more isolated. They never really work through a conflict; they use cutoffs as their means to "resolve" the situation.

This happened to me when a lifelong friend suddenly dropped off the radar screen. Even though I sent many cards and placed many calls, I didn't see or hear from him for 20 years. I had no clue about what happened until one day an e-mail arrived. He wrote that he was an alcoholic and had cut himself off from everyone after starting to drink heavily. But now, he was working through a 12-step program to stay sober and writing to say how sorry he was that he had isolated himself. I was delighted to hear from him, though I had to admit that the cutoff had hurt deeply.

Cutoffs are almost never the way to go, except perhaps when there is a threat of violence. Even then, there may be a way to see the other person when others are present.

Your Reflections

- Take time out from a difficult relationship if you need a cooling-off period, and let the person know that you'll be in touch at some point in the future.
- Seek therapy if you feel it is warranted.

- Take a look at your own behavior and how it may be contributing to the toxic interactions.
- Bring in a mediator to work through the problem.
- Keep in contact through written communications if nothing else.

Your Assignment

Consider if there is someone who you have cut off. Consider the psychological cost of that cutoff. If it feels safe, consider how you might reconnect with that person. If it doesn't feel safe, consider talking with a professional about the relationship.

Assignment: Back to the Future

Write a letter to your younger self, focusing on advice you would give yourself three years ago. For example, if you are a college senior, write a letter to yourself as a college freshman.

Knowing what you know today, what advice would you give yourself about how to succeed, manage relationships, and care for your well-being?

Your Reflections

- Regarding managing relationships, what advice do you wish you had received four years ago?
- Regarding planning for your future, what advice do you wish you had received earlier?
- What is your advice to your younger self about managing your energy and time?
- What is the best advice you have ever received?

Your Assignment

Write a one-page letter to yourself with advice you would love to have had three years ago. Give yourself both positive feedback and instruction. Date this letter and refer to it from time to time.

CHAPTER EIGHT
Self-Discovery Step Seven: Define Your Mission and Core Values

From a Student

"One day, I randomly came across a message that had been posted on Pope Francis's Twitter account several years ago that struck me deeply."

'The world tells us to seek success, power and money; God tells us to seek humility, service and love' (Pope Francis, 2013).

"Until that point, I had never truly recognized how intently I was seeking the very things he described the world was telling me to, rather than what God desired for my life."

–L.H.

Draft a Personal Mission Statement

Mission is about a very big question: What are you here on Earth to do?

It's a question most of us ponder at some point in our lives, but it's one of the most difficult to answer. Surprisingly, many successful leaders do have an answer, and in the best cases there is strong alignment between what they are leading and what they perceive as their mission.

When I think of mission, I think of action:

- I am here to do something.
- I am here to act on the environment.

A mission is usually so big, it's rarely finished. It's not necessarily a goal to be achieved but more like a lifelong journey with an ending off in the distant future. It also isn't something you invent. More than likely, it's something that springs from deep inside, something you've been doing or an inclination you've had all along.

My mission is to make the world a better place by helping individuals and organizations reach their full potential. That sounds vague and immeasurable. Yet, for as long as I can remember, this is what I have been all about. It was my mission even before I could conceptualize the notion of a mission.

When there was racial tension in the high school I attended, I organized other students and we put together a student relations council to talk about and deal with the problems. That ability to bring people of different backgrounds together is something I've been dedicated to my whole life. I'm not sure where it came from, but it has always been part of my mission.

Recently the former Michigan football star running back Vincent Smith presented to my undergraduate class at the UM Ross School of Business about a nonprofit organization he has started. The students excitedly connected to his mission: to increase access to healthy foods, reduce juvenile crime and reduce violent behaviors through a gardening based intervention. Already, Vincent and his group of volunteers, which include many pro football players, have started gardens in Flint, Ypsilanti, and Vincent's home town of Pahokee, FL. Learn more about his project online at TeamGardens.org

Your Assignment: Draft Your Personal Mission Statement

As you get ready to draft your personal mission statement, ask yourself:

Why am I here on earth?

What are the things that have driven me since I was a young adult?

What actions have I taken to further my mission?

Here are some examples from student mission statements:

- Be the first in my family to graduate from college
- Provide for others
- Define an unmet need in society and affect it
- Teach financial literacy to kids in Detroit
- Increase opportunity and education for others
- Empower people from underprivileged groups
- Create a better life for my future family
- Be a role model to my family and under-represented communities
- Give someone an opportunity

- Increase the number of under-represented minorities in sciences
- Support the emotional needs of underprivileged youth
- Live a fulfilling life
- Connect underprivileged youth with sports

Give Back

"We are such spendthrifts with our lives," actor and philanthropist Paul Newman once told a reporter. "The trick of living is to slip on and off the planet with the least fuss you can muster. I'm not running for sainthood. I just happen to think that in life we need to be a little like the farmer who puts back into the soil what he takes out."

Who will really know why some succeed and some do not? Regardless of the circumstances, those who find themselves successful, whether by accident of birth or by their own hard work, fully distinguish themselves by giving back to the communities and societies from which they come.

To be a truly successful leader, you have to be like that farmer and put the seed back into the soil. Newman started camps for children with serious illnesses and began a food company that gave its profits to nonprofit organizations. He was a beacon for what successful leaders can do if they focus on giving back.

I have met many leaders who are willing to give of themselves in appreciation for their success and in gratitude to society. Giving back has become more important to them than their initial success in business or industry.

They have started food-gathering organizations to collect the surplus from restaurants for the hungry. They have rebuilt some of the worst parts of the worst cities in Michigan. They have gone to Africa to help governments treat AIDS. They have adopted needy children and started projects to collect the stories of genocide survivors. They have helped the victims of September 11 identify lost family members through DNA matching.

I believe this current generation of young professionals will distinguish themselves as the giving generation as they often give while they are securing a stable income or launching a career. My son Daniel, when in early late 20s, went to Thailand to help rebuild communities devastated by the 2004 tsunami. My cousin David, when in his 20s, worked in Ethiopia to help children born with cleft palates. Numerous young adults work on political campaigns. All over America and throughout the world, people are making a difference by giving back.

Your Reflections

- Ask yourself: What am I doing today to give back?
- As you become more successful, what is your dream about how to give back to society?
- How will you plant the seeds today to replenish what you have been given in life?
- How will you teach your children the importance of giving back?
- What example are you setting for your children and coworkers about the importance of giving back?

Your Assignment

"During my time at Michigan, I've put this expectation on myself that after graduation I need to work in a large city for a well-known corporation and make a lot of money. This class has broken down that expectation. I determined that I want to do something that involves directly working with and helping other people...I also realized that I don't need to make a lot of money, just enough to that I can pay off my student loans in a reasonable amount of time."
–G.D.

Write your own statement about how you plan to give back. What inspires you. Will you give time, money, something else? By when do you plan to do this? Will you need the permission or support of others to do this?

Define Your Core Values

Your core values are the things that guide you, that you stick with no matter what. They may be as simple as, "I'm always going to tell the truth" or "I'm always going to respect others." They are the principles you abide by and vow not to compromise. Sooner or later you will be in situations where a course of action isn't clear. These values will guide your actions.

Your list of core values should include statements about what you will and will not do in conducting your life. They serve as a guide to your decision-making and attitude formation. Without core values as a guide, it is easy to lose your way personally and professionally.

Here are some examples of individual core values:

- Stay true to my faith.
- Show the love I have for the people in my life.
- Encourage people to succeed at their highest values.
- Set the right values for my company and my family, and adhere to them.
- Always tell the truth, no matter how difficult.
- Never inflict physical or emotional violence on another human being.
- Recognize the good in others.
- Always uphold my sense of integrity and adhere to my ethics.

Oprah Winfrey articulated the importance of living by your core values in these words: "Real integrity is doing the right thing, knowing that nobody's going to know whether you did it or not."

Your Assignment

List the five core values by which you already are living your life. (If you have three or seven, that's ok).

Remember, you do not have to invent your core values, you really just need to describe who you are already.

Here are some tips from Dr. Vic Strecher on how to think about your core values, from his book *Life on Purpose: How Living for What Matters Most Changes Everything.*

Select three to five words or phrases that describe the core values that are most important to you

Think about what you would hope people would say at your memorial service. What phrases might they use to describe you? What do your actions show about who you are?

Add your core values to your Personal Development Plan.

CHAPTER NINE
Map Your Lifestyle Values

From a Student

"As a college student I mainly focused on one end goal: doing well in class to eventually land my dream job. Dr. Rob helped me realize I will be much happier and healthier if I take a more holistic approach to achieving this goal. He helped me find a balance and set achievable short term goals for other aspects of my life, both personal and health related."

–a student

Establishing Your Balance Points

"I arise in the morning torn between a desire to improve (or save) the world and a desire to enjoy (or savor) the world. This makes it hard to plan the day."
–E.B. White

Like White, we get out of bed every day facing a host of choices. There is no one-size-fits-all formula for how we order the day or lead our lives. Each of us must decide what will sustain us, taking into account our energy, values and passions.

My students hope to have an impact—and not only at work. They realize it's not enough just to have a title on the door. They want to have influence in civic life or in a faith-based or social network or movement. They want time to take care of their bodies and their souls, and they don't want to be strangers in their own homes. The challenge is to find a way, every day, to balance these arenas, even in small ways.

No matter what the setting, it's important for leaders to be in tune with those around them. You can't be a lone wolf. You can't do it all by yourself. If you try to operate without the support of the pack, you're not likely to survive. This is especially relevant for today's two-career families, where it's harder than ever to keep the home fires burning. Research shows that women still carry more than their fair share of the responsibility for child care, taking care of the extended family and handling household duties.

The most effective people are multidimensional. They're not pedal-to-the-metal types who do nothing but work for the bottom line. They're energetic and driven, but they're able to shift nimbly from one arena to the next—and that helps to establish balance points. They work intensely, and they rest intensely. They get things accomplished, but they don't expend all of their energy in one area to the detriment of others. And they don't try to do everything at once. They may not balance out every day, but they do it over time.

Here are examples of what successful people do to buoy themselves as they seek balance.

Develop Supportive Routines

- Real estate developer Peter Allen starts his day with a glass of fresh-squeezed orange juice, online reading of more than a half-dozen newspapers plus the home-delivered New York Times, a special mix of five kinds of cereals with fruit and yogurt and "lots of thinking." That sets the tone. "After a day at the office," he says, "I still have the energy to teach a class, play golf or tennis or have a wonderful time with the grandkids."

- John Baldoni, a leadership consultant and coach, uses his morning exercise routine to think about what lies ahead for the day. "Running regularly, coupled with lifting weights, gives me the energy I need to think critically as well as creatively," he says. "I also augment my fitness regimen with golf, which I often play by myself. Walking the course gives me plenty of time to think and reflect and in the process gain insight into the challenges of the day."

- Yoga practice helps Bob Galardi, an executive coach, not only relieve pain and sore muscles but control stress. He uses calm-inducing yoga breathing before heading into a stressful situation.

Integrate Home and Work Schedules

- "I enter all the kids' schedules (soccer, swimming, school plays etc.) into my work calendar and make a point to schedule travel and other meetings so that I can attend at least two or three events per week—even if that event is picking them up from practice," says Kit Dickinson, president of an information technology company. "The car rides home are a great opportunity to connect with the child and hear how their day went or anything else they want to talk about."

Be Realistic

- "There are always times when work projects overwhelm life and life responsibilities trump work. The only way to avoid these balance swings is to either not have a life or not have to work," says Marisa Smith, an entrepreneur and partner in an information technology company. "Since neither of these is an option for us, we prefer to be realistic about the fact that there will be days when things will be out of whack. Managing our own expectations helps keep our frustration levels lower and enables us to maintain perspective until the pendulum swings back in the other direction."

Take Small Steps

- Planning guru Alan Lakein, author of *How to Get Control of Your Time and Life*, advocates using a five-minute rule if you can't seem to get started on a project. Set a timer for five minutes and work on the project. When the timer goes off, move on to something else or set the timer for another five minutes. Most people keep going for much longer than five minutes.

- I counsel clients to identify the time of day when they do their most creative work, then to keep that time free of meetings and distractions.

Ask Questions

- Rick Reid, an account development manager for an office furniture company, advises having the courage to ask others in your life—spouse, coworkers and friends—how you are doing as a husband, colleague and friend. "It can produce powerful revelations and the possibility of change that can bring about better balance overall," Rick says.
- Deborah Orlowski, an internal consultant for a university, was amazed when one of her clients seemed to heal so quickly after her husband's death at a young age. Her client shared: "We never left anything undone. When we were angry, we fought and got over it. We told each other we loved each other. We played together. We shared. Sure, I would have loved more time with him, but I have no regrets because there is no guilt...Nothing was left undone." That conversation changed Deborah's life. Now, she strives not to leave anything important undone or unsaid.

Examine Your Motives

- As Rick Reid says: "We are driven in our culture to succeed and to have more. I am just coming to grips with this in the past few years in my own life. How many others are also—those with 3,500-square-foot homes and Hummers in the driveway? How many really get that 'less is more'? ... If our society were not driven by the constant accumulation of money, how might that change the way we live? I like money and enjoy what I can do with it, but it does not rule me."

Happiness Is....?

Ever seen the Snoopy book "Happiness Is..."? My favorite line back then was, "Happiness is a warm puppy", but then I was an only child who dreamed of having a dog. Now, I still love a warm puppy, but I have a different take on happiness. Today I believe **happiness is having a good family life, good health, and a good job**.

By family, I mean having significant close relationships. I find that for most people, if they are not happy with their key relationships, they are generally unhappy in many aspects of their lives.

By health, I mean both physical and mental, and yes, I do believe they are inextricably connected.

By a good job, first and foremost I mean having a job. Being out of work creates misery. The next step would be having work which combines your passions with your unique talents in a healthy work environment.

So, how do you achieve all three? Due to time constraints, these three pillars of happiness often compete for your attention and energy. Furthermore, in a couple relationship, one person's interests can compete with the other person's interests.

Getting all of this in balance is a monumental struggle. Then, just when you think you have it figured out, something happens that throws off the balance. Every couple I know has struggled to sustain the right balance. Those who have succeeded have stayed together, and frequently, those who have failed, break up.

So based upon forty-three years of marriage and practice as a psychologist, here is some advice on achieving and maintaining happiness in a family relationship:

- Have visions of success in all three realms: Family, Health, and Career.
- Communicate your individual visions of success with your partner and discuss how you can achieve your dreams together. Revisit these visions over time, through life stages.
- Build trust and honesty in your key relationships. If you do not trust one another, you cannot be happy or successful.
- Communicate every day on how you are progressing toward your desired future.
- Recognize that you will face many adversities along the way. Some can be expected and anticipated, while others will catch you by surprise. Either way, having faith in yourself and your relationships will enable you to adjust your plan and achieve happiness.

Your Assignment

Consider what happiness looks like to you. Write three paragraphs.

Your vision of success in family. Think forward to the end of your life, when you look back with satisfaction. What do you see?

Your vision of health success. What does a healthy life look like to you? What do you need to do to achieve or maintain good health?

Your vision of career success. What does career success mean to you? What do you need to do to prepare yourself for the future you seek?

Ask When Enough is Enough

Some people compulsively compare themselves to others; they never think about what is enough in terms of their own satisfaction. They figure they need to strive for more, more, more—instead of recognizing that they already may have more than ninety percent of the people on the planet. They never stop to ask themselves: Is this how I want my life to be?

It's not just about money. It can be about achievement or prestige. It can even be about toys. I've got a perfectly good iPhone. It does everything I need it to do. But when a new iPhone comes out, what do I do? I need to stop and think: Do I really need it? Do I need to spend on a new toy? And how long before the next new toy comes along?

I usually use junky pens because I lose them right and left. But a friend once gave me an expensive pen because he thought it would better fit my station in life. I was terrified I would lose the pen, and sure enough, it vanished soon after he gave it to me. But I couldn't tell him that, so I went out and bought a replacement. The status symbol had become a kind of burden.

Your Reflections

- Get in the habit of comparing yourself downward as well as upward. Think about how much more you have than others.
- Travel to poorer parts of the world. It will help you appreciate what you have. Don't just go to the resort in Jamaica; drive around and see how ordinary people live.
- Don't just give money to a charitable cause—get close to the people it serves. Work at the

shelter or the food bank; don't just send a check. Take your kids along.

- Remember where you came from. Always appreciate how far you've come—and how far you have to go.

Your Assignment

Contemplate your relationship with symbols of success, such as material goods or status. For material things, do you take pride in quality or do you prefer to live lightly? Do you aspire to a big house, a fancy car, an exotic vacation? Do you hunger for recognition and attention?

Write up your philosophy on what success means to you. How much is enough for you in possessions, in accolades or job titles.

Then, think about what your family wants for you, what your friends and perhaps a romantic partner sees as your potential. Do they match? How will you negotiate their expectations and your goals?

On Money

Many of us have been raised with the idea that money will make us happy.

Personally, I was taught by my parents that any unhappiness they experienced was caused by a lack of money. They were raised in the Great Depression and they experienced hardship and fear of becoming impoverished.

When I was raised after World War II, economic times were good in our country. There was no longer a reason to fear that lack of money would cause severe problems. Yet, my parents passed on their fears to me, even though our circumstances were very different from their childhoods.

Research on happiness shows that beyond a minimum amount of money to keep us fed and housed, additional money does not make us any happier. There is not a strong correlation between the amount of money we make and the level of happiness we experience. Yet, we still operate under the myth that making a lot of money will be the key to happiness

How much money you want to make will be an important determinant of what career path you pursue.

Your Reflections

- Do you expect to support your extended family with the money you make?
- Do you currently have a lot of debt? If so how much of it is from your education, and how much of it is consumer debt? How much money will you have to earn to pay off your debt? If it is consumer debt what can you do to stop becoming more in debt? Have you

considered that you may have a spending problem?

- Have you taken some time to think about how much is enough?
- Have you talked to a financial planner about how much you need now and how much you will need in the future?

How to Get Paid for What You Love to Do

If you know your passions, strengths, and values, you may have identified your career path. Now the tough part, who will pay you to do what you want to do?

- Explore how much money is enough for you.
- If you're in a relationship, review with your partner your assumptions about how much is enough.
- Assess your financial risk-tolerance. How anxious you get when there's no secure path for making money every month? Entrepreneurial activities are not for those who are uncomfortable with risk-taking and require a steady paycheck.
- Who will benefit from what you do, whether it's a product to make or a service to provide? It's not about whether you value what you do, but it's about whether your client or employer values and needs your service or product.
- Determine whether the service or product you develop will relieve someone else's pain. Remember: people will pay much more readily to relieve pain than to seek pleasure.
- These days, people are also willing to pay for exceptional experiences. Creative types need to think about how they can create a great experience which will be valued in the market-place.
- Look beyond money to the important resources of time and energy. For some people having adequate time is more important than having a lot of money.

There's no easy answer for who will pay you to do what you love to do. If you are passionate enough, apply your talents enough, network enough, maintain relationships with people who will support your progress, and remain true to yourself, the chances are good you will find a way to make an adequate living. Remember, you will be facing difficult challenges and needing to call upon your very best self to achieve your dream. Those who commit to pursuing their dream often find unexpected resources to help them along the way.

Balancing Act Exercise

When I work with my clients, I often use an exercise, a precursor to setting goals, that helps them zero in on areas needing work.

The exercise goes like this:

1. Imagine that you are at the center of a personal ecosystem.
2. Surrounding you are five circles, symbols of the main spheres of influence in your life.
3. Now, draw a line from the SELF in the middle to each of the spheres. If the relationship is strong and there are no major issues, draw a solid line. If the relationship is strained in some way, or you feel there is unfinished business or some minor problem, draw a dotted line. If the relationship has a serious problem, draw a jagged line.

When people do this exercise honestly, they can quickly pinpoint areas where they have tension and stress. The next step is to set goals or an action plan to address the problems.

In one case, a man who was estranged from his son initially refused to take the first step to patch things up. But once he realized that waiting for the son to contact him wasn't going to work, he decided to take the initiative. He realized that he probably owed his son an apology and that that would go a long way toward drawing them back together.

In another instance, a man who was both overweight and a smoker used many excuses to ignore his problems. He couldn't stop smoking because he feared he'd gain more weight, and he couldn't exercise because the effects of smoking would leave him winded. To break the do-nothing cycle, I suggested he first consult a doctor. He finally did and discovered there was a medication that could help him quit smoking.

Almost anything can be resolved if you isolate the problem and set a course of action. Acting will make you feel better immediately. But if you remain in denial and do nothing, chances are the problem will eat away at you.

Your Assignment

Draw the circles. Draw lines between the "self" and the other circles.

Write up a paragraph about each connection. For instance, describe your relationship with work. Is there a solid, dotted, or jagged line? Consider why and what you will do to maintain (if positive) or fix (if strained) this relationship. Do this for all five spheres.

CHAPTER TEN
Describe Your Career Sweet Spot

From a Student

"Ultimately what I gained from this course was an adjusted set of goals as well as the tools and framework to achieve those goals. They are to: 1) get into medical school, 2) succeed at my upcoming job (meaning that I perform well and continue to expand my network professionally), and 3) remain healthy and maintain my relationships with my friends and family to achieve a tolerable work/life balance.

"Following the identification of my strengths, I began to reassess my career aspirations around them. I felt I needed to go into a career path that I will not only be successful at, but will also provide me fulfillment. Thus, I felt certain that following my year of work in finance, pursuing a medical degree is fitting. Not only will it allow me to utilize my strengths and fulfill my desire to be successful at things, but it is also morally appealing. The ultimate purpose of this career path is to provide care and care for the well-being of others."

–Laith Hasan

Find Your Career Sweet Spot

The sweet spot exercise is designed to help you find and occupation which will provide you the maximum happiness in your life. To determine the sweet spot, you need to fill out the following chart in your Personal Development Plan.

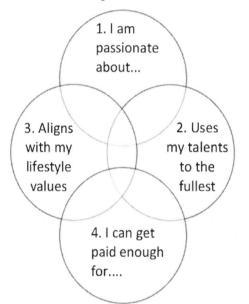

To fill out the chart you need to refer back to the sections of this book on your strengths, passion, values, and money. For each of the sections, summarize your findings and fill out the appropriate sections on this chart.

Next look at your career options and think about which option best combines your answers in each section. You may find that three sections are for fulfilled by a certain career choice, while one maybe not so much.

In circle number one, Lateesha knew that she was passionate about dance and helping young people develop their dancing skills. In circle number two, she felt that dancing and teaching dancing to others would use her talents to the fullest. For her, the key value in lifestyle was to be home with her child during non-school hours. Financially, she wanted to make enough money to contribute one half of the total needed to live in a neighborhood near her family.

However, while she found that dancing fulfilled three of the four circles: passion, talent, and values, she could not meet the financial expectations of her partnership with her husband.

So Lateesha had a series of conversations with her family about what to do about her love of dancing. Since she had an entrepreneurial bent, she looked into starting a business in her town. It turned out that no one was teaching jazz dance which was becoming very popular. She decided to rent space and start a jazz dance studio where she taught young people how to dance. She also created a dance troupe where she was the lead dancer.

Through this creative solution she was able to dance for herself, teach others to dance, and make enough money by having other instructors come into her studio to be able to develop the career she desired.

By doing her sweet spot exercise, she was able to discover a creative solution that enabled her to do what she loved, what she was good at, what aligned with her values, and what provided adequate financial return.

Your Assignment

Draw four overlapping circles. Label the first circle "I am passionate about." Put what you are passionate about in the circle. Label the second circle "Uses my talents to the fullest." Put what would use your strengths and personality to the fullest in this circle. Label the third circle "Aligns with my lifestyle values" Put your primary lifestyle values in this circle. Label the fourth circle "I can get paid enough for." Put what matches your financial needs there.

What is the overlap?

CHAPTER ELEVEN
Envision Your Success

From a Student

"My vision 10 years down the line is to see myself as a successful researcher working in the R&D department of a company in my field of interest (Machine Learning and Computer Vision), while having enough free time to pursue my interests and to spend time with my family. I would also like to see myself to have traveled to many places around the world.

"The quote 'Success is not final, failure is not fatal, it's the courage to continue that counts' from Mike Klein was my biggest takeaway from the entire course."

–Sharath Nittur Sridhar

Describe Your Vision of Success

Ari Weinzweig, cofounder of Zingerman's Deli in Ann Arbor, Michigan, has one of the best approaches to formulating a vision that I've seen. He speaks about it and has written it up in his book, *A Lapsed Anarchist's Approach to Managing Ourselves (Zingerman's Guide to Good Leading)*. He believes that while your mission and vision should be compatible, they aren't the same. In his view, a mission is global in scope and never-ending. A vision is a mental picture of success, time-constrained, inspiring and specific enough that it can be measured.

To figure out your vision, Weinzweig advises answering this question:

When you're really successful at a point in the future, what will that success look like?

To help you peer into the future:

- Employ sensory-based images: What would success physically look like? What would it feel like?
- Let your vision inspire. It should get your juices flowing.

Why create a vision?

- It allows us to create reality instead of just reacting to present-day problems.
- It's a statement of optimism about the future.
- It forces us to act on the reality that there is no safe path.
- It makes us hold ourselves accountable.
- It tells us what we aren't going to do.

Once you have your vision, Weinzweig says you should write it down and, of course, communicate it to others.

Your Assignment

Imagine yourself five years from now.

Close your eyes and think about how you want your life to be. Where do you want to be living? Imagine the particular view you have out of your window. Look around and see what is in your space. Next imagine who are you living with? Are you by yourself? With roommates? With a partner? What are the quality of your relationships?

Now imagine you are at your work setting. Where do you dream you will be working? What will you be doing while you are at work?

Next, shift to your free time. How will you be spending your time? What will you be doing to enjoy yourself? What will you be doing to take care of yourself? How will you be dealing with the obstacles that typically get in your way?

As you write your vision, describe what you are actually seeing, hearing, and feeling. Be sure to make it vivid and inspiring.

Your vision should be the fulfillment of your dreams, what you hope for in the future. A vision is something to dream of and aspire to.

CHAPTER TWELVE
Set Your Goals and Harness Your Willpower

From a Student

"My goals have been almost constantly changing throughout this course, as I tend to take every day as it comes and not plan too far into the future. This course has taught me the merit in having a 12-month plan and has forced me to think ahead more concretely than I ever have before. I am confident that critical thinking and self-reflection skills that this course has taught me will allow me to successfully finish out my last semester at Michigan, and will continue to help me as I make my way into the working world...No matter what happens, I know I will continue to rewrite my own story and will be sure to make adjustments to the plan as necessary while keeping my overall values, ethics, and mission in mind as I do so."
–Cailin O'Donnell

Create Your Goals

"Before taking this course, I knew that opening a restaurant was one of my major life goals. However, I had not put as much thought into how I would go about achieving this goal, nor did I think about the people and lessons that would help me get there. Taking this course, and completing this Personal Development Plan, has been very effective in providing clarity as to the action steps needed for my personal and professional success. Opening my restaurant will not be possible without obtaining my degree, earning and saving adequate funds, developing my network, and creating a sound business plan. Hopefully, following these steps will put me on the right path to opening my own business within the next 5 years."
–a student

For most of my life, I've used a simple goal-setting method that I learned from a colleague as a young man. I write my goals on index cards using this format:

- **What?** The specific, measurable goals that I want to achieve and the date that I set them. (No vague dreams.)
- **By when?** The date for achieving the goals. (Research shows that 90-day goals can be most effective. Longer-term ones tend to get lost; shorter-term ones come to resemble to-do lists.)
- **Why?** The reason why each goal is important. What values are central to the goals?
- **How?** The process, step by step, that I will use to achieve each goal.
- **Support?** The people I will work with to achieve each goal.

I like this system because it's intuitive. It follows the questions your brain would naturally ask: What do I want to do? How fast am I going to get it done? Why do I want to do it? How will I get it done? Who will help me?

Your plan doesn't have to be hugely detailed, but you do need a plan. I have a whole box of goal cards going back to 1968. As a reminder of the goals I've set, I carry a folded-up index card in my wallet listing them. I add and cross off as I go.

You can find more detailed goal-setting approaches, but this low-tech version is easy and effective. And it's easily adaptable to our microchip-driven world. Feel free to make your shoebox full of goals a digital one.

Your Assignment

Write out the short- and long-term goals that will get you the next steps towards your lifetime vision. Define their what, by when, why, how, and describe the support you will need to achieve them.

Prioritize and make a plan for each goal. Consider what might keep you from achieving these goals and make plans to address perceived obstacles. Write these out in your Personal Development Plan.

Who? Pick Your Support Team

"While I consider myself to be a person who always wants to lend a hand in helping others achieve their goals, I find that I am reluctant to reach out to others for the same help. By gaining a better understanding of people within my support system, and how I can leverage them for assistance and accountability in achieving my goals, I am more confident in my own ability to achieve those goals with their help."
–H.M.

One of the myths that people often hold dear is that they are responsible for their own success. But today, there is more and more acceptance of the notion that if you are going to succeed, it will be within a community, a group of other committed souls.

We shouldn't be surprised at this. Think about the great innovators and doers in history. Were they operating solo? Was Thomas Edison working alone in his lab? Was Michelangelo up on the scaffolding all by himself, day in and day out?

People seek out and rely on social connections to a far greater extent than they did even a few decades ago. Think about the success of online networking sites like LinkedIn and Facebook. If you accept that most things are accomplished with a "posse," it's clear that you must think about who will accompany you on your journey, who will support you and help fill in the gaps. This takes on even greater importance during bad economic times. If you lose your job, your network might help you find a new one. Isolated people have a much harder time of it. Your network needn't just be online. Yours might be your bowling league or your investment club or those you worship with.

Be Realistic

From a student:

"Originally, my definition of success was a bit more audacious because it included me having a thriving business within five years and I really thought that was feasible. However, through this class, I learned that in order to enhance self-management, I need to be aware of faulty thinking and recognize that being overconfident, like I was, and ignoring vulnerability can lead to bad action"
–a student

It's important to be realistic when you set goals—to pick things that you have some reasonable expectation and probability of achieving. You don't want to set a goal of playing basketball in the NBA when you didn't even make your high school team.

Goals also should be specific and measurable. Don't plan to change your personality or something fundamental about you; rather, it's about altering your behavior so you can reach the goal. So, focus on things that you can control. (Realize, too, that you can't control someone else's behavior, though you can control your reaction to what they do.)

The Serenity Prayer is useful to keep in mind as you set goals. What are you hoping or praying for? Are you seeking the courage to set a goal or should you be aiming for something short of that—a "serenity goal" of acceptance and the courage to deal with a problem or issue on that level?

Break down your goals into achievable steps. Your goal may be to run a marathon. The first step might be to run daily, any amount. Then, you might build up your runs to longer distances. Each step should take you closer to your ultimate goal.

And finally, when you do succeed at one of your goals, enjoy your success. Reward yourself. Buy something you've wanted. Take a trip you've been meaning to take. Do something that gives you a pat on the back and brings a smile to your face.

Your Reflection

Review your vision and goals you have created so far.

- Are there ways you should edit them to make them more realistic?
- Build in a few intermediate milestones where you plan celebrations to mark your progress.
- Share them with a trusted friend or family member and ask for their feedback on them, including the realism of your timelines.

Willpower and Goal Setting

Usually when we think of willpower, we think about resisting short term pleasure for long term gain. However, I believe sustained willpower is what is required to achieve long term goals.

My friend and coaching client Kathleen Craig's story illustrates this principle. When she graduated from high school, Kathleen started college with the goal of achieving a bachelor's degree. However, as often is the case, life showed up. Within a few years Kathleen got married, started her family, and began a career working full time.

Although these events presented obstacles, Kathleen never lost sight of her goal to graduate. After over a decade, she returned and received her degree from EMU. Not only did she reach that goal, but she also created a new goal and launched a business. The company has created an app that helps teach financial literacy to children. Since they have already sold their product to several banks, she was recently able to give up her day job to work full time on the company.

I recently asked Kathleen how she found the willpower to keep going in the face of so many challenges. Here are a few of her keys to success:

- She kept motivated by remembering that she wanted the goal, not only for herself, but also for her children **(Find a strong motivator)**.
- She never allowed herself to imagine that she would not achieve the goal **("NO" is not an option)**.
- She used her willpower to stick to a strict schedule for studying, Sunday and Monday evenings and after the kids went to bed at 8:00PM **(Be disciplined in scheduling specific times to work on your goal)**.

- She would only allow herself to watch TV if she studied during the commercials. Inevitably, she would get going and realize she needed to turn the TV off in order to properly focus. At least this would get her going, when all she really wanted to do was have leisure time. **(Sometimes you need to trick yourself into getting started).**
- She relied on the support of a community which included her parents, five brothers and sisters, and her husband. It didn't hurt that she was motivated to be the first of her siblings to graduate from college. **(It takes a community, and maybe sibling rivalry, to achieve a long term goal).**
- She always acts now and not later, getting things done as soon as possible rather than waiting until they have to be done. **(Have a "Now List" rather than a "To Do List").**
- Wherever she worked, she made time to study and use her employer's training, mentoring, and coaching resources. **(Use the resources available and don't be afraid to ask for help).**
- The path was not continuous, but she always kept her eye on the goal. **(Hit "pause" but never "stop").**

Fear: Trust Your Gut or Do It Anyway?

Last week I talked with a friend who had an offer to pursue an opportunity which he had always desired. However, at the moment of decision, he found himself hesitating and fearful of making the commitment. Fortunately, before he turned down the option, we had an opportunity to discuss his feelings and decision-making process.

Like many opportunities, this one came along at the wrong time. He was already at the limits of his capacity, both physically and mentally. Yet, this was something he had always wanted to do and normally would have jumped at the opportunity if it had come at a different time. To complicate matters further, he found his confidence wavering at his ability to succeed at the new endeavor.

We talked about the challenge from many perspectives. The following perspectives might also be useful to you when you next experience self-doubt about something important you would like to achieve:

- We examined what it was he feared, and why he was lacking confidence in this matter, even though he was generally a confident person.
- We talked about worst-case scenarios: If what he feared happened, did he believe he would be able to cope with it? Could he deal with the possibility of failure?
- How would he feel if he passed up the opportunity and it never came around again?
- If he were to take on the challenge, what resources could he call upon to ensure success?
- How had he been able to deal with similar challenges in the past? What inner and

external resources had he called upon to enable him to face and overcome his fear?

After thinking through these questions and talking to other people who knew him well, he made the decision to take on the challenge. Will he be successful? Only time will tell. Based upon his track record of success, he will probably find a way to succeed in this activity as he has done with other activities like it in the past. But, as is the case whenever taking on a challenging risk, he may not succeed. However, he's comforted by the fact that he will be able to cope no matter what the outcome.

Boost Your Resilience

Resilience is the ability to rebound from hardship, difficulty and misfortune and successfully adapt to adverse situations. It's perhaps more important today than ever, because the world is more interconnected than at any time in history. This interconnectedness means we experience turmoil faster, more intensely and more often.

Nothing great in life is ever achieved without taking considerable risk and facing distinct difficulties.

So, going forward, it's important to understand how you have handled adversity in the past. That's the best predictor of how you will handle it in the future.

Your Reflections

- How accurately do you assess the risks in challenging situations?
- Where would you place yourself on the cautiousness scale—over or under?
- Do you tend to be excessively optimistic or pessimistic?
- Does risk cause you to charge forward or retreat?
- Do you set realistic but challenging goals?

Tips

- Carefully decide what you can control and what you can't. Focus your energy on the former.
- Keep perspective on your ultimate goal—for example, to save as many jobs as possible to ensure the company's survival, to raise sensitive children, to have a happy marriage.

- Remember, there are always other solutions. Find ways to improvise and stay flexible.
- Avoid succumbing to temptations to quit, to cheat, or to exploit.
- Keep yourself inspired: read, discuss, pray; do whatever it takes.
- Look for humor, even when the situation looks bleak.
- Remember and honor your personal stories of overcoming adversity. Find time to take care of yourself on a daily basis.
- Acknowledge fear and find a way to tame it.
- Make the tough decisions and do not look back.
- Commit to overcoming adversity—to win and not to allow yourself to fail.
- Be realistically optimistic but stay grounded in reality.
- Accept responsibility for past failures but do not beat yourself up over it.
- Find a small group of people who are willing and able to support you.
- Cast off negative people.
- Define specific, winnable goals.
- Communicate the facts, no matter how bleak.

CHAPTER THIRTEEN
Create Your Personal Development Plan and Graduate

Personal Development Plan

Throughout the course of their careers, successful people develop and manage a growing network of high-quality professional relationships with multiple bosses, peers, a host of colleagues up and down their organization, customers, clients, and others. Ultimately, professional success is a function of how well you manage these relationships over the long-term.

The centerpiece of this self-guided course is for you to create your own Personal Development Plan from the exercises in this book. Your plan will articulate a meaningful professional goal and outline a plan to achieve it. It should explain what support you need from others and how you plan to get it. When you feel you've finished, I suggest taking a half hour to present this plan to someone you trust.

Your Assignment

Review your answers from the Self-Discovery Exercises in your Personal Development Plan.

Review your Occupational Sweet Spot.

Detail your vision.

Describe your goal:
What? Describe the specific, measurable goal you want to achieve. It can be a professional goal, or a personal development goal that you connect to professional success. The goal must be something you will achieve after the end of the semester, but no longer than 12 months into the future.

By when? Set a deadline for achieving your goal. Describe success in specific detail. When you achieve your goal, what will success look like? What will success feel like?

Why? Explain why this goal is important to you personally. What core values are central to this goal? What passions will you be able to engage working toward this goal? How is this goal grounded in your mission?

How? Describe in as much detail as possible how you will achieve this goal. How do your strengths align with this goal?

Support? One of the myths that people often hold dear is that they are solely responsible for their own success. But today, there is more and more acceptable the notion that if you are going to succeed, it will be within a community, a group of other committed individuals. What support do you need from others to achieve this goal, and how will you get it?

Your Plan of Action:

Describe in detail the specific actions you will take to achieve your goal. You should have 3-5 specific actions. If achieving your goal requires buy-in or actions/decisions from others, then you should include an action about how you will persuade them to support you. Present these actions in a timeline, showing when each action will be taken, as well as major milestones along the way.

Key Insights and Takeaways:

Communicate the key insights and takeaways you had in the course of doing this assignment – about yourself, your work, etc.

Final Assignment: Commit to Action

My Parting Thoughts for You

Thank you for participating in this process. Here's a quick summary of what I think is important and what I wish for you.

- Find the correct balance between these two opposites: accept and love yourself as you are, yet constantly seek ways to make yourself even better.
- Beware of your negative self-talk. You can teach yourself to "look on the sunny side of life" even if you were not raised to do so.
- Know your strengths and build on them.
- Recognize your blind spots and commit to being aware of them.
- Consider the "why." Before thinking about your goals, think about your life mission. Think about why you are here on Mother Earth.
- Create a vivid vision for what you would like your life to look like five years from now. Make it so compelling that you can experience it through all five senses.
- Set specific short-term goals that align with your mission and will move you forward toward your vision. Write each of your goals down on an index card, and then keep the cards close. For each goal, answer the following questions: By when? What is the specific goal? Why is it important? How will you go about achieving it? Who will support you?
- Learn to say your name clearly and with confidence. When you introduce yourself, spell your first name so people will remember it. Likewise, make a real effort to

remember the names of those you are fortunate to meet.

- Be kind to everyone, especially your FRIENDS, FAMILY and TEAMMATES.
- Find a great mate with whom to share your life. We are social beings. Finding a partner will enhance your life in every way. You need not wait until your career is established. Likewise, with friendships: the quality of your friendships will be the key to your happiness in life.
- Conceive of a dream and believe in it. Once you have achieved it, conceive of another dream. Keep doing this throughout your life.

The reason I wrote this book is that my dream is to help young people. I believe this book will help you implement these eleven teachings. I wish you all the best.

Oy, The People You'll Meet!

My favorite graduation speech is not actually a speech at all. It is a delightful book written by Dr. Seuss when he was 87: *Oh, the Places You'll Go!*

Although I'm not yet 87, and I am never going to be as wise as Dr. Seuss, I'd like to share a few lines I've written as advice for graduates.

Oy, The People You'll Meet!
Congratulations, today is your graduation day,
Over the next few years you'll meet some fascinating people along the way.

Happy or sad you can choose to be,
It's the quality of the relationships that will set you free,

Some people will be interesting,
Some will be nice,
Some will treat you cold as ice.

Some people you'll meet will love to compete,
Don't be scared!
It's them you can defeat.

Some will become friends,
You can learn to get along great,
Nothing better than to collaborate.

Some will have so many ideas,
They will drive you nuts.
Others will cherish the rules
And refuse to accept any
"Ifs, ands, or buts."

So get out there and meet every type!
But beware of the ones with too much hype —
Or who blame you for their lousy state,

Or who want to get high with you on the very first date.

Or who dare you to do things, cause "you'll never get caught"
Or who shame you and make you feel like toxic waste...
You get the point, the ones who leave you with a bad taste.

So next time you're in a coffee shop or bar,
Put your damn phone down and look around.
Say "Hello!" with a smile —
Your future best bud might have just walked in from afar.

Resources

Bradberry, Travis and Jean Greaves. *Emotional Intelligence 2.0.* San Diego, CA: TalentSmart. 2009.

Buckingham, Marcus and Donald Clifton. *Now Discover Your Strengths.* New York: Gallup Press. 2001.

Collins, Jim. *Good to Great: Why Some Companies Make the Leap...and Others Don't.* New York: HarperCollins. 2001.

Goleman, Daniel; Richard Boyatzis and Annie McKee. *Primal Leadership: Learning to Lead with Emotional Intelligence.* Boston: Harvard Business School Press. 2004.

Gottman, John and Nan Silver. *The Seven Principles for Making Marriage Work.* New York: Three Rivers Press. 1999.

Isay, David. *Listening Is an Act of Love: A Celebration of American Life from the StoryCorps Project.* New York: Penguin Press. 2007.

Lakein, Alan. *How to Get Control of Your Time and Life.* New York: Signet. 1974.

New York Times. *Portraits: 9/11/01.* New York: Times Books. 2002.

Pasick, Robert. *Awakening from the Deep Sleep: A Powerful Guide for Courageous Men.* New York: Harper Collins. 1992.

Pasick, Robert. *Conversations with My Old Dog.* Canton, Michigan: David Crumm Media, LLC. 2009.

Pasick, Robert. *Balanced Leadership in Unbalanced Times.* Canton, Michigan: David Crumm Media, LLC. 2009.

Pausch, Randy with Jeffrey Zaslow. *The Last Lecture.* New York: Hyperion. 2008.

Quinn, Robert E. *Building the Bridge as You Walk On It: A Guide for Leading Change.* San Francisco: Jossey-Bass. 1996.

Quinn, Robert E. *Deep Change: Discovering the Leader Within.* San Francisco: Jossey-Bass. 1996.

Rath, Tom. *StrengthsFinder 2.0.* New York: Gallup Press. 2007.

Rath, Tom and Donald O. Clifton. *How Full Is Your Bucket? Positive Strategies for Work and Life.* New York: Gallup Press. 2004.

Strecher, Vic. *Life on Purpose: How Living for What Matters Most Changes Everything.* New York: Harper Collins. 2016.

Weinzweig, Ari. *Zingerman's Guide to Good Leading, Part Three: A Lapsed Anarchist's Approach to Managing Ourselves.* Ann Arbor, Michigan: Zingerman's Press. 2013.

Weinzweig, Ari. *Zingerman's Guide to Good Leading, Part Four: A Lapsed Anarchist's Approach to the Power of Beliefs in Business.* Ann Arbor, Michigan: Zingerman's Press. 2016.

Personal Development Plan

You may download your Personal Development plan template as a Google doc online: goo.gl/NIWVzu

You will need to copy the document so that you can edit and customize your plan.

Editor: Dunrie Greiling, Ph.D.

Dunrie is a marketing and operational consultant, writer, and editor. She works with technology startups and makes her clients' websites more rich and more discoverable. She received her doctorate in Biology from the University of Michigan.

You can learn more about Dunrie's work at ScientificInk.com

Other Books by Dunrie

Internet Marketing Start to Finish: Drive Measurable, Repeatable Online Sales with Search Marketing, Usability, CRM, and Analytics (with Catherine Juon and Catherine Buerkle). 2011.

Author: Robert Pasick, Ph.D.

"Dr. Rob" is an executive coach, organizational psychologist, and a lecturer at the University of Michigan Ross School of Business and at the University of Michigan's Center for Entrepreneurship at the College of Engineering.

Rob has been practicing in the Ann Arbor area as a clinical & organizational psychologist and executive coach since he earned his Ph.D. from Harvard University in 1975.

Rob has appeared on "Oprah" and "The Today Show." He is the founder and host of Leaders Connect, which provides monthly Leaders Connect Breakfast networking events and Leadership Roundtables to the community.

Visit RobPasick.com for weekly blog posts and videos from Leaders Connect events.

Other Books by Dr. Rob

Men in Therapy: The Challenge of Change (with Richard L. Meth). 1990.

Awakening from the Deep Sleep: A Powerful Guide for Courageous Men. 1992.

What Every Man Needs to Know. 1994.

Pet Loss: A Death in the Family. 2003.

Balanced Leadership in Unbalanced Times. 2009.

Conversations with My Old Dog. 2009.

Made in the USA
Lexington, KY
10 January 2017